Advance Praise for *Faucian Bargain*

"Steve Deace is a true patriot whose zeal for liberty is undeniable. Every day, Steve walks the walk when it comes to fighting for Americans' fundamental rights. This book is written with a keen understanding of the pain and devastation we've all seen throughout this pandemic. Throughout, Steve's passion for protecting Americans' freedoms is ever-present."

—U.S. Senator Ted Cruz (R-TX)

"In his famous Farewell Address, President Eisenhower warned about allowing public policy to become captive to a scientific elite without regard to the principles of our constitutional system and the goals of a free society. Eisenhower was prescient. During the COVID crisis, states like New York that embraced unadulterated Faucism saw poor results across the board, while states that pursued an Eisenhower-style approach like Florida protected freedom and performed better in education, economy and health outcomes. Executives are elected to lead and make tough decisions, and such leadership cannot be outsourced to health bureaucrats like Fauci."

—Florida Governor Ron DeSantis

"In this important book the authors do the job our uninquisitive media has failed to do throughout this ordeal. Confirming with cited and sourced details the enemy of both liberty and logic the lockdowns have proven to be. Which also proves too much power in the hands of an unelected bureaucrat, regardless of his intentions, can no longer be our new normal."

—U.S. Senator Rand Paul (R-KY)

"This is an important book, to both get answers to how we got here and to help us never succumb to something like this ever again. Permitting unelected bureaucrats to hold this much power indefinitely doesn't end well."

—**Mark Levin,** *New York Times*
bestselling author and talk show host

"In their typical fashion, Steve Deace and Todd Erzen spare no expense in pursuit of truth. We've been told a lot of things during this pandemic, and a lot of them contradict each other. This book uses documented data and sources to cut through the clutter, most of it Fauci's, and bring us to a place of reason and science."

—**Glenn Beck,** *New York Times* bestselling
author and Radio Hall of Fame broadcaster

"This book is needed to help us end this statist charade once and for all. The data clearly shows we can both protect the most vulnerable and restore our liberties. But for that to happen we need to follow the actual science, and not a liberal-media-created celebrity such as Fauci."

—**David Limbaugh,** *New York
Times* bestselling author

"Seekers and followers of truth are in short supply during this unprecedented time in American history. Steve Deace ruthlessly seeks the truth, reveals what he finds, and backs it with evidence and data. He's written my kind of book, one that challenges prevailing corporate media narratives."

—**Jason Whitlock,** former National
Journalism Award winner

"*Faucian Bargain* shines light on the deception Americans faced at the hands of Tony Fauci's twisted power. As a country, we allowed Fauci and his media enablers to utilize our fear of the unknown to push through Leftist ideology and suffocate our freedoms. This book is a must-read for those who seek the truth."

—Former U.S. Senator Jim DeMint,
Chairman of the Conservative Partnership Institute

"This timely but sadly necessary book lays bare the truth about Dr. Anthony Fauci, for Americans to fully grasp the tyrannical devastation he inflicted on our great nation. From Fauci's glaring contradictions, to his raw abuse of power in shutting down the greatest economy in the world, this book demonstrates with precision the lesson we must take from this travesty. Never. Again."

—Congressman Chip Roy (R-TX)

"It didn't take some of us long to figure out something wasn't quite right with Dr. Anthony Fauci. It took him months before he acknowledged the public-health consequences of lockdown. He was dead wrong on schools. He warned that Florida was 'asking for trouble,' and yet Florida ended up doing better than states Fauci praised. Steve Deace and Todd Erzen have been tracking the whole fiasco from the beginning, and *Faucian Bargain* is their urgently necessary corrective to the mainstream narrative of the heroic Fauci."

—Tom Woods, *New York Times* bestselling author

"This book is a weapon of mass destruction against the dumbest decision I've ever seen—lockdowns—and the general of Covidstan, one Anthony Fauci. May it be read and heeded, so we never fall for such a scam again."

—Jesse Kelly, talk show host

"Rahm Emanuel famously said, 'You never want a serious crisis to go to waste.' Steve Deace and Todd Erzen masterfully expose how appeals to 'trust the experts' and 'trust the science' helped Anthony Fauci fulfill Emanuel's wish. The 'experts' win, but the American people lose—bigly."

—**Josh Hammer,** *Newsweek* opinion editor

"One would be hard pressed to think of anyone in government who's done more lasting damage to the country than Dr. Anthony Fauci. Emboldened by a media in full swoon and his own ego, Fauci inflicted untold pain and devastation across the country without a hint of remorse. Few people saw through his façade of faux expertise from the start—Steve Deace was one. For a year, Deace helped expose Fauci's self-serving careerism, his terrible unscientific advice, and the long-term consequences of Faucism. This book will serve as an historical account of one of the country's worst years and the man most responsible: Anthony Fauci."

—**Julie Kelly,** American Greatness

"The American public needs the truth about Dr. Fauci, and this book lays it out all out here in all its horrifying detail. Fauci has become a star, ignoring science in favor of propaganda. We follow his advice (and the advice of bureaucrats in general) at our own peril. If you want the truth, it's all here in a compelling and easy read. But be forewarned...the truth will make you very angry."

—**Mark Meckler,** President, Convention of States Project

FAUCIAN BARGAIN

The Most Powerful and Dangerous Bureaucrat in American History

STEVE DEACE and TODD ERZEN

A POST HILL PRESS BOOK
ISBN: 978-1-63758-198-8
ISBN (eBook): 978-1-63758-112-4

Faucian Bargain:
The Most Powerful and Dangerous Bureaucrat in American History
© 2021 by Steve Deace and Todd Erzen
All Rights Reserved

Cover art by Cody Corcoran
Cover Photo by Yuri Gripas/Abaca Press/Bloomberg via Getty Images

This book contains research and commentary about COVID-19, which is classified as an infectious disease by the World Health Organization. Although every effort has been made to ensure that any medical or scientific information present within this book is accurate, the research about COVID-19 is still ongoing.

Post Hill Press
New York • Nashville
posthillpress.com

Published in the United States of America

Table of Contents

Dedicated to our children, and the next generation. May we pass on to them whatever is left of the American Dream.

Introduction

"A Republic, If You Can Keep It"

According to legend, upon exiting the Constitutional Convention—where the now eighty-one-year-old Ben Franklin had just successfully lobbied his fellow Founding Fathers to ratify the US Constitution—he was confronted by a group of citizens wondering what sort of government the delegates had given these new United States of America.

"A republic, if you can keep it," Franklin is said to have famously answered.

In other words, his generation had fulfilled its mission. It was now time for a new generation to answer history's call to fulfill theirs, with independence already boldly declared and then successfully defended. These colonies were now free and independent states, further codified into law by the passing of the Tenth Amendment one year after the Constitution itself, which states:

The powers not delegated to the United States by the Constitution, nor prohibited by it to the States, are reserved to the States respectively, or to the people.

Those twenty-eight words were the final words written into the Bill of Rights, which were the very first amendments to the Constitution. They are merely twenty-eight words, but they pack a wallop. For they reinforce, once more both bluntly and plainly, the original premise of our Constitution that makes it unique in all of human history—this governing document was meant to limit the power of the federal government, not the freedom of those it governs.

As a generation, the Founding Fathers had two things in common—a reverential fear of God and a fear of too much power placed in the hands of fallible/fallen human beings. One of the textbooks popular during the years when many of them were being educated was called *Cato's Letters*. It is full of admonitions like this one:

The love of power is natural. It is insatiable, it is whetted, not cloyed by possession. Power renders man wanton, insolent of others, and fond of themselves.[1]

Enter Anthony Fauci.

Cato's Letters is not a book of prophecy but of history, though we will argue in the book you're about to read that

---

[1] Allan Brownfield, "A Theme for the Bicentennial: The Founding Fathers' Fear of Power," Foundation for Economic Education, October 1, 1974, https://fee.org/articles/a-theme-for-the-bicentennial-the-founding-fathers-fear-of-power/.

excerpt is a brutally perfect description of Fauci's ongoing reign. Its authors were not sages peering into a crystal ball foretelling our future, or the rise of the most powerful and dangerous bureaucrat in American history in our time.

Rather, they knew long before George Santayana did that those who have not learned from history are doomed to repeat it. They were not drunk on Utopian notions about the nature of man. They accepted the realization there are forces at work within the creation beyond us, that we are not the ultimate power down here. They also accepted the biblical notion that "all have sinned and fallen short of the glory of God" as a mission statement for our species, which an accurate reading of history continually (and sadly) reinforced.

Therefore, the Founding Fathers they helped mentor understood there was an ironic tension in their central claim: on the one hand they sought to overthrow a king's power, but on the other (if successful) they knew better than to now claim that same power for themselves—lest they become like that which they despised.

The great George Orwell was similarly not a prophet, but as an astute observer of history he understood history not only repeats but it often rhymes. He, too, recognized that revolutions—particularly when the goal is the empowering of the state but merely under different wannabe despots or do-gooders this time—often turn out to look a lot like that which they had just overthrown.

The final line of his classic *Animal Farm* sums it up perfectly:

The creatures outside looked from pig to man, and from man to pig, and from pig to man again; but already it was impossible to say which was which.[2]

Another textbook the Founding Fathers learned much from was the Good Book itself. Jewish history and Mosaic Law, or the "Old Testament," was influential and often cited throughout their writings and public discourse, residual evidence of which still exists throughout our nation's Capitol to this day. One of the pivotal moments in Jewish history as told in the Old Testament ironically comes during the only book that doesn't specifically mention God by name—Esther.

Esther is the Hebrew wife of Xerxes the Great, the most powerful man in the world at the time as the king of the mighty Persian Empire. Such a vast and powerful state was too much for a singular man to run, so it required a similarly vast and powerful bureaucracy to maintain it. Not even a ruler as wise and empathetic as Solomon could rule over so much by

---

[2] George Orwell, *Animal Farm: A Fairy Story* (London: Secker & Warburg, 1945).

himself, let alone one from a line of ruthless conquerors such as Xerxes.

And yet at the exact same time King Xerxes is making a young Jewish girl the star (Esther literally meant "star" in Farsi) of his kingdom as his new queen, the Jewish people she came from are existentially threatened. Not so much by King Xerxes himself, but by his administrative state. Specifically its de facto prime minister Haman, who was manipulating his influence within the bureaucracy as a means to plot a genocide of the Jewish people. That plot is only successfully foiled when Esther risks her own life to disclose it to King Xerxes before it is hatched.

One of the great works of modern fiction is J. R. R. Tolkien's *The Lord of the Rings*, where even the Dark Lord Sauron requires bureaucracy to maintain his hold on power from behind his Black Gate. Whether it's the rings he forged himself to hold the various kingdoms of Middle Earth in line, or his servant Saruman dispatching the vile Wormtongue to be the true tyrannical power behind King Théoden's rotting throne.

That makes it a clean sweep. Scripture, history, philosophy, and fiction all tell the cautionary tale of a bureaucracy (or a singular bureaucrat) gone wild.

However, one nation's bureaucracy is another nation's "checks and balances." When the Founding Fathers established three independent branches of government with their eighteen enumerated powers, as well as thirteen distinct and independent state governments complete with all their various local and community infrastructures, they were not intending to create an administrative state of perpetual unelected bureaucracy. The very assertion that you were a nongovernmental organization come to solve a current social or political issue—with ample taxpayer funding, of course—would've gotten you tarred and feathered in their midst.

Instead, they desired layers of liberty insurance. It was precisely because they didn't trust human nature as a basic instinct that they sought to create layers of competitive accountability. Meaning "we the people" would have multiple peaceable options on the table to have the rule of law upheld, our God-given rights maintained, and our liberty prized. And each of these layers would be a check-and-balance on the other, because the competitive tension among them would disincentivize consolidation towards despotism.

Yet all it takes for "checks and balances" to become bureaucracy, and bureaucracy to devolve into an all-powerful and self-perpetuating administrative state, is for self-governing men and women to do nothing. There is no government system that can sufficiently restrain the fallen nature of man once man no longer acknowledges he is fallen.

Unfortunately, recent generations of Americans have not answered history's call but rather kicked the can down the road. Thus setting the stage for a problematic figure such as Fauci to emerge as the most powerful and dangerous bureaucrat in American history. Figures such as Fauci are rarely the cause but the effect of the culture from whence they came. Only in the last fifty years or so of American history would it be possible for an uber-crat like Fauci to be conceived.

In his farewell address back in 1961, President Dwight Eisenhower warned we were poised to be held hostage by a celebrity class of allegedly infallible experts:

Today, the solitary inventor, tinkering in his shop, has been over-shadowed by task forces of scientists in laboratories and testing fields. In the same fashion, the free university, historically the fountainhead of free ideas and scientific discovery, has experienced a revolution in the conduct of research. Partly because of the huge costs involved, a government contract becomes virtually a substitute for intellectual curiosity. For every old blackboard there are now hundreds of new electronic computers. The prospect of domination of the nation's scholars by Federal employment, project allocations, and the power of money is ever present and is gravely to be regarded. **Yet, in holding scientific research and discovery in respect, as we should, we must also be alert to the equal and opposite danger that public policy**

could itself become the captive of a scientific-technological elite.[3] [emphasis added]

The bad news is we not only didn't heed Ike's warning, but succumbed to it. The good news is there's still time to do something about it. For if a book such as this can be freely written and read, then we still have enough freedom to push back.

This book will not argue that COVID-19 isn't a serious disease or that coronavirus isn't a serious pandemic. But it will not exaggerate the seriousness, either. We, the authors of this book, believe the truth is its own reward, and the truth should be set free to have its say. So it will be stated, and cited, in bold colors and not pale pastels. But while even far more vicious contagions such as the Spanish flu eventually come and go, the tyrannical precedents set by this current one threaten to remain long after it's a threat.

Thus threatening whatever is left of our constitutional republic.

Nor will this book seek to turn Fauci into a real-life caricature of a Goldstein or Snowball. His name is on the

---

[3] "Transcript of President Dwight D. Eisenhower's Farewell Address (1961)," ourdocuments.gov, https://www.ourdocuments.gov/doc.php?flash=false&doc=90&page=tra nscript.

marquee, yes, but the truth is he's not really the main villain. Fauci is not some sinister figure who cynically manipulated these events in order to rise to power. As you will see in this book, he contradicts himself way too much, and is too easily exposed, to be considered that sort of mastermind. He's more Apple Dumpling Gang than Nicolae Carpathia.

Fauci is not the disease but the symptom. He's the construct of the Matrix, at worst an Agent Smith if you will, not the Matrix itself. For our federal leviathan to exist and sustain, it requires multitudes of figureheads such as a Fauci. And if Fauci weren't there to step to the microphone, it would've just been someone else.

The likes of Fauci within the DC swamp are, well, *legion*.

That's because we have been derelict in answering history's call. Largely because prior to coronavirus we were drunk on comfort and complacency. But COVID-19 has taught us, harshly, that all we've been blessed to take for granted and which previous generations had to fight for can be taken away faster than you can say "nonessential business." That even here, in twenty-first-century America, you can wake up one day and toilet paper is not only rationed, but the local business that sustained your family for decades can be erased from memory. That the local church that brought grace and mercy to the community can be shuttered. That funerals, graduations, weddings, proms, and other rites of passage that testify to the fact life is more than a mere survival rate can be cancelled with no makeup date promised.

A republic if you can keep it.

To that end, this book sees the role it has to play in such a cause as arming you, the reader, with the most devastating weapon of our current technological age—information. Some of this information is so important, and will be so foreign to the Fake News narrative/panic porn you've been bombarded with, that it will need to be repeated. Just as the COVID vaccines emerging at the time this book was written require more than one dose, so will some of the truths you'll come to learn in this book.

Whosoever controls the flow of information in any culture ultimately has control. We will use this book as a compilation of information, all true and all sourced, that allows you to practice true self-government. Each of you reading this, if we do our jobs, will now have the power of information in your hands. Power to wield to your city councils while debating more flat-earth, voodoo mitigation efforts that have repeatedly proven not to work. Or your state legislatures, your governors, your members of Congress, and so on. Once you've read this book, everyone who claims to rule you will be without excuse—but so will you.

Do not simply read this book and then say "cool story, bro." This book is a weapon but not just against Fauci as a person as much as what he represents. For if we don't stop this now there will be others like him in the future, and they may not even pretend to be as charming as he does. If you're afraid of the power you've seen displayed by this man none of us voted for, and who many of us didn't even know existed just two years ago, you're right to be. But fear all the more the prospect that Fauci, if unchecked, will be the baseline for whatever comes next. And rest assured, something wicked this way comes.

Here, and no further. The line must be drawn here. The answer is us.

A republic, and we must keep it.

Chapter 1

A Man of Many (Contradictory) Opinions

To begin our trek down the rabbit hole we have assembled a simple chronicle, all cited, of Anthony Fauci's varied opinions on COVID-19. But be warned, they're so varied they're not so simple to follow.

In fact, the good news about being led by such a malleable, all-powerful bureaucrat is if you don't like a current take Fauci has on the virus and accompanying public policy, stick around because it's likely to change…and change…and change some more.

So come and see for yourself how Fauci has felt strongly about every side of every coronavirus issue.

We begin in January 2020, when Fauci appeared on local radio in New York City to say we had nothing to fear from the virus except fear itself:

It's a very low risk to the United States. It isn't something the American people need to be frightened about.[4]

Later that month, Fauci confirmed what science has previously learned about respiratory outbreaks—that contrary to science fiction they're not driven by hordes of asymptomatic carriers who then go out and zombify an unsuspecting populace (remember this Fauci quote for later on in this chapter):

Even if there is some asymptomatic transmission, in all the history of respiratory-borne viruses of any type, asymptomatic transmission has never been the driver of outbreaks. The driver of outbreaks has always been a symptomatic person.[5]

Then on February 28, 2020, Fauci yet again struck a similar "just relax" tone while writing in the prestigious *New England Journal of Medicine*, in which Fauci compared COVID-19 to the—gasp!—flu:

---

[4] J. Edward Moreno, "Government Health Agency Official: Coronavirus 'Isn't Something the American Public Need to Worry About," The Hill, January 26, 2020, https://thehill.com/homenews/sunday-talk-shows/479939-government-health-agency-official-corona-virus-isnt-something-the.

[5] Richard Harris, "As China's Coronavirus Cases Rise, U.S. Agencies Map Out Domestic Containment Plans," National Public Radio, January 28, 2020, https://www.publicradiotulsa.org/post/chinas-coronavirus-cases-rise-us-agencies-map-out-domestic-containment-plans#stream/0.

If one assumes that the number of asymptomatic or minimally symptomatic cases is several times as high as the number of reported cases, the case fatality rate may be considerably less than 1%. This suggests that the overall clinical consequences of Covid-19 may ultimately be more akin to those of a severe seasonal influenza (which has a case fatality rate of approximately 0.1%) or a pandemic influenza (similar to those in 1957 and 1968) rather than a disease similar to SARS or MERS.[6]

March 8, 2020, just a few days before the country shut down, Fauci told CBS News "there's no reason to be walking around with a mask." CBS went on to report:

While masks may block some droplets (from spreading the virus), Fauci said, they do not provide the level of protection we think they do. Wearing a mask may also have unintended consequences: people who wear masks tend to touch their face more often to adjust them, which can spread germs from their hands.[7]

---

[6] Anthony S. Fauci et al., "Covid-19—Navigating the Uncharted," *New England Journal of Medicine*, February 28, 2020, https://www.nejm.org/doi/full/10.1056/NEJMe2002387.

[7] Jonathan LaPook, "How U.S. Hospitals Are Preparing for COVID-19, and What Leading Health Officials Say about the Virus," *60 Minutes*, March 8, 2020, https://www.cbsnews.com/news/coronavirus-containment-dr-jon-lapook-60-minutes-2020-03-08/.

Definitely remember that inconvenient truth for later in this book.

And now, we come to March 11. The day the earth stood still. The day our way of life ended, with no definitive hope of when it might return. For that is the day Fauci testified before Congress that COVID-19 would be "10 times more lethal than the seasonal flu."[8] This is the statement that sent shockwaves across the country and launched us into lockdowns. The NBA, the most lucrative American pro sports league playing games at that point, shut down the next day. A day later, so did the NCAA Tournament—perhaps the most popular collegiate sporting event in the country.

And Fauci gave this stark, panic-inducing testimony just three days after going on national television to declare masks were dumb. Just eleven days after comparing the fatality rate for COVID-19 to a bad flu in perhaps the nation's most renowned medical journal. By the way, what changed in those eleven days? What new piece of evidence or data did Fauci acquire to inspire such an about-face? That is a question we will explore later on in this book.

For now, let us continue down Fauci's trail of tears.

---

[8] Noah Higgins-Dunn and Berkeley Lovelace Jr., "Top US Health Official Says the Coronavirus Is 10 Times 'More Lethal" Than the Seasonal Flu," CNBC, March 11, 2020, https://www.cnbc.com/2020/03/11/top-federal-health-official-says-coronavirus-outbreak-is-going-to-get-worse-in-the-us.html.

March 16, 2020, Fauci helped launch us into the "15 days to flatten the curve" that only flattened the health care system instead. This effort was based on the now-disgraced Imperial College doomsday model,[9] which probably requires a whole other book to adequately deconstruct. How wrong was the Imperial College model about what COVID-19 would do to America? We ended up so successfully flattening the curve to preserve our hospitals from being overrun with COVID patients, that by early May millions of jobs had been lost in the...wait for it...wait for it...health care sector![10]

At the end of those fifteen days, with our health care system still not overrun except for a handful of cities, Fauci convinced President Trump to extend a national shutdown for another thirty days.[11] Fauci and company based most of their case for extending the national quarantine on the always-wrong Institute for Health Metrics (or IHME) model, which other experts from Harvard and even former IHME committee

---

[9] Peter Aitken, "Imperial College Model Britain Used to Justify Lockdown a 'Buggy Mess,' 'Totally Unreliable,' Experts Claim," Fox News, May 16, 2020, https://www.foxnews.com/world/imperial-college-britain-coronavirus-lockdown-buggy-mess-unreliable.

[10] Margot Sanger-Katz, "Why 1.4 Million Health Jobs Have Been Lost during a Huge Health Crisis," *New York Times,* May 8, 2020, https://www.nytimes.com/2020/05/08/upshot/health-jobs-plummeting-virus.html#:~:text=Published%20May%208,%202020%20Updated%20May%2010,%202020,nearly%20recession-proof:%20a%20buffer%20against%20the%20business%20cycle.

[11] Billy Perrigo, "President Trump's Advisors 'Argued Strongly' against Easing Coronavirus Measures Too Early, Anthony Fauci Says," *Time*, March 30, 2020, https://time.com/5812439/trump-coronavirus-measures-fauci/.

members called "not well-suited" and a "travesty."[12] So this is fine.

For example, on April 1, 2020, the IHME model predicted our home state of Iowa would be at 1,300 deaths on April 30. But in mid-May of 2020 the state was at just 271 deaths. It predicted Georgia's peak death day would be 134 victims on April 21, yet only 24 people ended up perishing that day. Much like the Imperial College model, you could also write an entire book on just wrong IHME Model coronavirus projections alone.

However, after enslaving the country to these flawed and failing models, Fauci told Fox News in mid-April of 2020[13] that he's always been skeptical of them! You can't make this stuff up!

At what point here was Dr. Fauci right about anything? When was he wrong? You're guess is as good as ours, because in the first four months that coronavirus was on our radar, when it was vital we have a sober-minded gathering of as much uncorrupted and unbiased information as possible to set

---

[12] Sharon Begley, "Influential Covid-19 Model Uses Flawed Methods and Shouldn't Guide U.S. Policies, Critics Say," STAT News, April 17, 2020, https://www.statnews.com/2020/04/17/influential-covid-19-model-uses-flawed-methods-shouldnt-guide-policies-critics-say/.
[13] "Fauci: Real data trumps any coronavirus model," Fox News, April 10, 2020, https://video.foxnews.com/v/6148686950001?fbclid=IwAR0ouoZHlEifv9Z4Th 0Eeq28P16s6Vh5I1fCysxg7zMyplNMWb5iSQHhwqA#sp=show-clips.

the stage for a firm public policy, Fauci went from one extreme to the other and all points in-between.

Unfortunately, at the same time Fauci was being promoted by both the media and the White House—perhaps the only time those two entities agreed on anything the entire four years Trump was president—as our infallible guide never to be questioned, only to be followed. Thus, instead of fighting for his job after so many inconsistencies during such a critical time, Fauci's public persona was actually gaining critical mass.

But as the months of Fauci contradictions and waffling droned on, Barstool Sports founder Dave Portnoy spoke for an increasing number of Americans with this viral rant:

What the (expletive) is going on? When did this become "flatten the curve" to "we have to find a cure or everyone's going to die"? [Fauci] gets in front of the Senate, he's like, we reopen the country it's quick everyone's dead! Where'd that come from? Find a cure? Who says we're gonna find a cure? We haven't found a cure for cancer. It took AIDS 20 years—and do we even have a cure? So the economy is just shut down? If you told me because of corona I lost Barstool and had to start over, I'd rather die of corona, seriously, or at least take my chances. You can't just make everyone stay inside and basically start [their lives] over. It's insane. There are no great options, but you can't decimate an entire economy.[14]

Senator Rand Paul has also scrutinized Fauci foibles during his past Senate testimony. As a doctor who was also raised by one, Paul is uniquely qualified to spot Fauci overreaches and distortions. Paul became so frustrated he said that Fauci "owes an apology to every single parent and school-age child in America"[15] for his initial resistance to kids going back to school, despite their safely returning to schools in dozens of countries around the world. Paul also exposed Fauci making panicked and false claims about the lack of crossover immunity from other coronaviruses to COVID-19.

Joy Pullmann of *The Federalist* didn't mince words in her analysis with the not-so-subtle title "five times Anthony Fauci proved he understands science as a tool to lie to Americans." Pullmann sets the stage by asking, "What is science? It is a search for demonstrable material facts. It's the process by which we validate observable natural processes. If Fauci acted as a scientist, he would clearly communicate what scientists

---

[14] Yaron Steinbuch, "Barstool Sports' Dave Portnoy Unleashes Profane Rant over Coronavirus Lockdown," *New York Post*, May 14, 2020, https://nypost.com/2020/05/14/barstool-sports-dave-portnoy-unleashes-profane-rant-over-coronavirus-lockdown/.

[15] Emma Colton, "Here Are Fauci's Biggest Flip-Flops and Backtracks amid the Coronavirus Pandemic," *Washington Examiner*, December 1, 2020, https://www.washingtonexaminer.com/news/here-are-faucis-biggest-flip-flops-and-backtracks-amid-the-coronavirus-pandemic.

have observed about Covid-19, which in many cases is the opposite of the panicked media narrative he helps produce."[16]

To bolster her case Pullmann cited five areas (in her words) where Fauci hasn't exactly been intellectually honest: 1) Singing in church not okay, protesting in the streets—I can't say; 2) "I have confidence in the U.K.'s rushed vaccine" (while telling Americans who get our vaccines they still must be treated like lepers anyway); 3) Endless double-dealing on school shutdowns; 4) Cloth masks don't work—except to control people; 5) Americans simply can't handle the truth (Fauci's self-justification for why he's not been honest at times). Pullmann's blunt conclusion is also a worthy summary of this book:

Fauci should have been fired long ago for his long history of failing to conduct and oversee effective scientific research while politicizing it, and for his open cheerleading of the utter destruction of American lives, hopes, plans, dreams, and freedoms so he can dance on America's funeral pyre while having CNN film it. Lockdowns of the healthy have long been known to be utterly ineffective at changing the course of

---

[16] Joy Pullmann, "5 Times Anthony Fauci Proved He 'Understands Science' as a Tool to Lie to Americans," *The Federalist*, February 23, 2021, https://thefederalist.com/2021/02/23/5-times-anthony-fauci-proved-he-understands-science-as-a-tool-to-lie-to-americans/#.YDUmE_i9tBg.twitter.

infectious diseases while imposing horrific costs. Fauci is therefore scientifically and morally bankrupt.[17]

Miranda Devine at the *New York Post* laid out in devastating detail how Fauci was originally against a key policy decision President Trump made that saved untold lives. She quotes former White House trade adviser Peter Navarro as saying Fauci was "adamantly opposed"[18] to Trump's ban on travel from China, which Fauci would later admit saved American lives.[19] Fauci also admitted to *InStyle* magazine in a glowing cover story that he lied on CBS News about not needing to wear masks, but it's totally fine because it was for the greater good as he sees it. He was concerned we'd run out of masks for health care professionals, Fauci said, so no regrets.[20]

---

[17] Pullmann, "5 Times Anthony Fauci."

[18] Miranda Devine, "Dr. Fauci Needs to Be Held Responsible for COVID-19 Mistakes: Devine," *New York Post*, January 24, 2021, https://nypost.com/2021/01/24/dr-fauci-needs-to-be-held-responsible-for-mistakes-devine/.

[19] "Dr. Fauci Credits Travel Ban with Saving Lives, Refuses to Specifically Blame Protests for Spreading COVID," Yahoo News, July 31, 2000, https://news.yahoo.com/dr-fauci-credits-travel-ban-012907036.html.

[20] Kevin Dietsch, "Fauci Says He Doesn't Regret Telling Americans Not to Wear Masks at the Beginning of the Pandemic," Business Insider, MSN, July 16, 2020, https://www.msn.com/en-us/news/us/fauci-says-he-doesnt-regret-telling-americans-not-to-wear-masks-at-the-beginning-of-the-pandemic/ar-BB16P84e.

Of course, this begs the question of whether there were any other times he felt justified in lying to us? Well, according to Senator Marco Rubio (R-FL), Fauci also "selectively lied" about herd immunity. In an op-ed he wrote for Fox News, Rubio said the following:

For most of this year, Dr. Fauci and other scientists in our public health establishment have been telling Americans that about 60 to 70 percent of the nation would need a vaccine in order for us to reach herd immunity and make the coronavirus a non-issue. But (later) Dr. Fauci admitted that he believes the real number is in fact significantly higher—perhaps 75 to 90 percent—and he declined to be forthright because he felt the country wasn't ready to hear it. Only now did he say that he feels he has the freedom to "nudge this up a bit" without discouraging the nation.[21]

Rubio then pulled no punches about the dangers of what happens when an unelected bureaucrat such as Fauci decides he alone is capable of determining how much truth the American people can handle:

The American people deserve the truth; they also deserve accountability. When elected representatives make decisions,

---

[21] Sen. Marco Rubio, "Sen. Marco Rubio: Dr. Fauci Lied about Coronavirus to Manipulate Our Behavior—That's Appalling," Fox News, December 30, 2020, https://www.foxnews.com/opinion/dr-anthony-fauci-coronavirus-marco-rubio.

they can be held responsible by the public. But when public health officials with decades of experience and leadership within our nation's institutions short-circuit the political process and make these decisions themselves, they deny the American people that same opportunity—and to change course if desired.[22]

Basically Rubio just summarized why we're writing this book.

Which brings us back to Fauci's comments rightly dismissing irrational fears of asymptomatic spread. Less than six weeks after Fauci previously told the country the truth, that asymptomatic spread is not a driver of respiratory outbreaks, Fauci took the lead on the national lockdown policy largely predicated on a fear of asymptomatic spread! What science changed during that time? The answer is none.

In fact, as the real-time data was confirming Fauci's original dismissal of asymptomatic spread fears after months of lockdown, [23] Fauci flip-flopped and falsely claimed

---

[22] Rubio, "Dr. Fauci Lied."
[23] Daniel Horowitz, "New Study Finds Weak Asymptomatic Virus Transmission," RealClear Health, August 20, 2020, https://www.realclearhealth.com/2020/08/20/new_study_finds_weak_asymptom atic_virus_transmission_280897.html.

asymptomatic spread was driving a "new phase" of the virus.[24] Further demonstrating how false his assertion was, data from the CDC claimed only 15 percent of *all* US COVID-19 infections thus far were asymptomatic.[25]

You don't need to be a decorated or celebrity expert to do the elementary math here. If only 15 percent of all COVID-19 infections in the US were asymptomatic, then it's mathematically impossible for asymptomatic cases to be the drivers of virus transmission. There simply aren't enough asymptomatic cases in the grand scheme of things for that to be the case. However, if asymptomatic spread is not a clear and present danger, then the whole rationale for locking down an entire country falls apart, so you can also do the motivational math from there, too.

We're not saying Fauci just gloms onto whichever narrative will expand or increase his authority and/or stature, whether scientifically valid or not, but we are saying there is an odd pattern of it looking like he does.

---

[24] Joshua Berlinger et al., "August 3 Coronavirus News," CNN, August 3, 2020, https://www.cnn.com/world/live-news/coronavirus-pandemic-08-03-20-intl/h_5b6d32b4c95ac8a2b02c12c98b323242.

[25] Alex Berezow, "CDC Estimates 83 Million U.S. COVID Infections. This Has Major Implications," American Council on Science and Health, February 9, 2021, https://www.acsh.org/news/2021/02/09/cdc-estimates-83-million-us-covid-infections-has-major-implications-15330.

Making matters worse is Fauci's willingness/desire to say literally whatever fueled the narrative he preferred at the time, which set the tone for how we're still being cynically patronized by the COVID intelligentsia even now at the time this book was being written. Look no further than how narratives began to miraculously change after Joe Biden was declared the 2020 election winner.

Call it the Biden vaccine:

- A peer-reviewed paper[26] from August 6, 2020, with positive things to say about the controversial coronavirus prophylactic hydroxychloroquine, which was panned and ridiculed by Fauci[27] after it was promoted by Trump as a viable treatment, didn't appear in the *American Journal of Medicine* until January.

- NPR was caught publishing two totally different narratives about COVID-19 the day before and the day

---

[26] Peter A. McCullough et al., "Pathophysiological Basis and Rationale for Early Outpatient Treatment of SARS-CoV-2 (COVID-19) Infection," *American Journal of Medicine* 134, issue 1 (January 1, 2021): 16–22, https://www.amjmed.com/article/S0002-9343(20)30673-2/fulltext.

[27] Chris Smith, "Dr. Fauci Contradicts Trump Once Again on Hydroxychloroquine," BGR, July 29, 2020, https://bgr.com/2020/07/29/coronavirus-cure-fauci-contradicts-trump-hydroxychloroquine-tweet/.

after Biden's inauguration.[28] The final day of the Trump presidency, NPR breathlessly noted the coronavirus "death rate accelerates." However, the day after Biden was inaugurated suddenly and spectacularly that same NPR went with the headline "Deadly U.S. Coronavirus Surge Has Peaked." Life comes at you fast, bro.

- Kansas's rare Democrat governor lowered the sensitivity threshold for a positive COVID test in her state.[29] After Biden won the election, of course.

- Maryland's anti-Trump Republican governor decided after Biden won the election it was time to reopen schools.[30]

- Washington, DC, decided a Biden presidency made it now safe to reopen bars and restaurants.[31]

---

[28] Eric (@IAmTheActualET), "That Was Fast," Twitter, January 21, 2021, https://twitter.com/iamtheactualet/status/1352425132330016771.

[29] Michael Austin (@KSTaxEconomist), "Here's the Exciting News," Twitter, January 21, 2021, https://twitter.com/KSTaxEconomist/status/1352373110771748870.

[30] Jason (@upthereworkin), Twitter, January 21, 2020, https://twitter.com/upthereworkin/status/1352398945805283332.

[31] Lucas Manfredi, "DC Mayor Bowser Confirms Indoor Bar and Restaurant Service to Resume at 25% Capacity Starting Jan. 22," Fox Business, January 21, 2021, https://www.foxbusiness.com/economy/dc-mayor-bowser-confirms-indoor-bar-and-restaurant-service-to-resume-at-25-capacity-starting-january-22.

- Massachusetts' anti-Trump Republican governor out-of-nowhere began easing coronavirus restrictions.[32]

- Chicago, of all places, started pushing back on teachers unions for not returning to work for in-person instruction.[33]

- New York Democrat Governor Andrew Cuomo amazingly clamored to reopen his state.[34]

However, a special place in the Hall of Shamelessness has to go to the World Health Organization, whose lack of clarity President Trump was so frustrated by that he defunded it. The WHO deserves dishonorable mention all by its lonesome, which is why we didn't include it in the above list, because this one takes the cake.

Literally one hour after Biden was inaugurated, the WHO decided to finally alert nations around the world that the sensitivity levels for determining a COVID-19 positive test

---

[32] Nik DeCosta-Klipa, "Charlie Baker Announces Plans to Lift Business Curfew and Nighttime Stay-at-Home Advisory," Boston.com, January 21, 2020, https://www.boston.com/news/coronavirus/2021/01/21/massachusetts-business-curfew-stay-at-home-advisory.

[33] Dawn Reiss, "Chicago School System Locks Out Some Teachers, Withholds Pay for Not Returning to In-Person Instruction," *Washington Post*, January 12, 2021, https://www.washingtonpost.com/local/education/chicago-schools-reopening-teachers/2021/01/12/3a2173d2-5508-11eb-a08b-f1381ef3d207_story.html.

[34] Mairead McArdle, "Cuomo Says New York Must Reopen Economy," Yahoo News, January 11, 2021, https://www.yahoo.com/now/cuomo-says-york-must-reopen-223303731.html.

were too high and to cease the focus on testing asymptomatic people.[35] In other words, the casedemic that led to so much of the panic porn used to justify locking Americans down, and shut down civilization globally, was now no more.

Just. Like. That.

Allow us to quantify for you what this meant in real-time. On January 8, 2021, or the first full day after the WHO recommended changing coronavirus testing metrics, the United States reported an all-time high in new daily cases of 295,121. Less than 40 days later on February 15, 2021, the United States was reporting a seven-day average of just 87,073 cases.

That represented a whopping 71 percent decrease![36]

This massive decrease came despite the fact the new vaccines were just beginning to emerge, and much of the US was mired in such a horrific winter even Texas was under a state of emergency.[37] You probably can't claim the WHO's

---

[35] "WHO Information Notice for IVD Users 2020/05," World Health Organization, January 20, 2021, https://www.who.int/news/item/20-01-2021-who-information-notice-for-ivd-users-2020-05.

[36] David Hogberg, "COVID-19 Cases Plunging Too Quickly to Be Credited to Vaccine Rollout," *Washington Examiner*, February 17, 2021, https://www.washingtonexaminer.com/news/decline-covid-cases-us-not-vaccine.

[37] "President Joseph R. Biden, Jr. Approves Texas Emergency Declaration," February 14, 2021, https://www.whitehouse.gov/briefing-room/statements-releases/2021/02/14/president-joseph-r-biden-jr-approves-texas-emergency-declaration/.

change of heart was the sole reason for it, given hospitalizations for COVID-like symptoms also suffered a steep decline, but you can't deny the coincidental timing of it, either.

Speaking of coincidence, it's hard to see this ominous pattern as simply one of those. It's too obvious, and therefore we know what that means.

The virus is very real. It has taken many lives. We must never lose sight of that.

That being said, the weaponization and politicization of this virus are also very real, and both were used to empower the likes of Fauci as well as threaten our way of life. Maybe even to determine the outcome of an election.

Near as we can tell, there're only two possible explanations for Fauci's role in this chicanery. He either purposely manipulated viral narratives and circumstances in order to assert his own authority. Or he's so bad at this, and/or such a BSer, it turns out he's just a big-mouth wannabe out over his skis while up against the worse pandemic in a half century.

Both possible explanations are bad.

Chapter 2

The Great Unanswered Questions

This book is intended to serve two primary purposes.

First, to arm its readers with the information necessary to reclaim the power that should belong only to we the people, and not unelected bureaucrats. Second, to do our part in making sure something like what has been done to our way of life never ever happens again.

To that latter end, we believe we need 9/11-type tribunals to get the answers to the following two questions:

How were we ever gonna flatten the curve if we didn't know when the curve began, and what caused Fauci to go from a calming force to sending the nation into a COVID-19 panic?

The reason these two questions are so important is because the answers to them will reveal the still unseen motivations that led to perhaps the dumbest management decision in American history—lockdowns. And no, it will not be enough to simply end the lockdowns, declare victory over the virus, and move on. We have permitted precedents to be set here that you can count on being used against us later. We have shown statists that if they show us a little bit of fear, we will roll over for them. Rest assured, unless we correct that mistake we will be asked to make it again.

The best way to fix that mistake is to find out, once and for all, whether it was a mistake. While the authors of this book believe in the tradition of limited government and individual liberty established by our Founding Fathers, we do not believe in no government whatsoever. We acknowledge there are vital roles a civil society needs fulfilled that are difficult for individuals to perform on their own, and therefore the corporate action of government is necessary (such as the military, law enforcement, border security, etc.).

We also acknowledge this is an imperfect world, which includes circumstances beyond our control and forces that cannot be easily subdued. Therefore, it is entirely possible that one day an unprecedented contagion could threaten us at such an existential level, drastic government action will actually be required. The authors of this book are staunchly for the sanctity of human life, and to that end do not believe we have a right to not have our desires be inconvenienced when the sanctity of life is at stake (see seat belt laws, laws forbidding narcotics, etc.).

However, early on the data indicated COVID-19 was no Captain Trips, and yet Fauci's fetish for lockdowns has continued right up until the time this book was being written. We must know why.

On July 24, 2020, a little more than five months after "15 days to flatten the curve" was launched, the Kaiser Family Foundation released a study that found "eight of 10 people who have died of Covid-19 were 65 or older."[38] Even earlier than that, the CDC reported the median age of Americans who sadly died of COVID-19 between February 12 and May 18, 2020, was 78 years old—which is also the average American life span.[39] On the other hand, the median age of the average American worker is more than 30 years younger at 41.9 years-old.[40] So why then did we let millions of Americans lose their jobs and businesses, when the typical American worker was nowhere near the age of those overwhelmingly most likely to succumb to coronavirus? Why did we quarantine millions

---

[38] Kaiser Family Foundation, "8 in 10 People Who Have Died of COVID-19 Were Age 65 or Older—But the Share Varies by State," July 24, 2020, https://www.kff.org/coronavirus-covid-19/press-release/8-in-10-people-who-have-died-of-covid-19-were-age-65-or-older-but-the-share-varies-by-state/.

[39] Jonathan M. Wortham et al., "Characteristics of Persons Who Died with COVID-19—United States, February 12–May 18, 2020," July 10, 2020, Center for Disease Control, https://www.cdc.gov/mmwr/volumes/69/wr/mm6928e1.htm.

[40] US Bureau of Labor, "Median Age of the Labor Force, by Sex, Race, and Ethnicity," last modified September 1, 2020, https://www.bls.gov/emp/tables/median-age-labor-force.htm.

upon millions who were decades away from the demo COVID-19 mostly kills?

To put a finer point on it, by Memorial Day of 2020 the CDC already knew the disease known as COVID-19 targeted our most elderly populations by an order of magnitude, and yet nine months later the week ending March 7, 2021, only 46.9 percent of American schoolchildren were back receiving in-person learning.[41] That very week, President Biden himself even assured a schoolgirl on national television, "Don't be scared. Kids don't get Covid often…the evidence so far is children aren't the people most likely to get Covid."[42]

What is the innocent explanation for this inexcusable disconnect? When you find it, let us know.

Examples like this are why we must get answers to the two questions in bold at the beginning of this chapter, and why getting those answers requires a 9/11-type tribunal. Otherwise we have no way of knowing for sure when the next public health scare that allegedly demands lockdowns comes, and we promise you it one day will, whether or not this is the real thing in the future. And they will use our fear of the unknown

---

[41] Phil Kerpen (@kerpen), Twitter, March 7, 2021, https://twitter.com/kerpen/status/1368573070500315145.
[42] Kate Sullivan and Paul LeBlanc, "Biden Reassures 2nd Grader Afraid of Getting Covid-19: 'Don't Be Scared, Honey,'" CNN, updated February 17, 2021, https://www.cnn.com/2021/02/16/politics/biden-town-hall-coronavirus-second-grader/index.html.

against us, with catch-phrases such as "are you really willing to take that risk?"

Instead, our Constitution was written to limit the size and scope of government. Which also implies it is government that must justify to us any further encroachment upon our liberty. The burden of proof is always on the bureaucrats. They are to serve us, not us serve them. We don't just take their word for it. We are to demand they show us the data that allows us to make an informed decision, and if they can't then the answer is no. History shows erring on the side of increasing government authority at the first whiff of unverified danger is not a recipe for lasting liberty.

So what did Fauci know, and when did he know it? On February 28, 2020, Fauci wrote the following about coronavirus in the prestigious *New England Journal of Medicine*:

> *If one assumes that the number of asymptomatic or minimally symptomatic cases is several times as high as the number of reported cases, the case fatality rate may be considerably less than 1%. This suggests that the overall clinical consequences of COVID-19 **may ultimately be more akin to those of a severe seasonal influenza** (which has a case fatality rate of approximately 0.1%) or a pandemic influenza (similar to those in 1957 and 1968) rather*

than a disease similar to SARS or MERS, which have had case fatality rates of 9 to 10% and 36%, respectively.[43] [emphasis added]

If you're wondering where the much-panned talking point "coronavirus is just a bad flu" originally came from, this is it. It didn't come from those rascals at QAnon or some MAGA Reddit forum. It first came from none other than Fauci himself. However, just eleven days later while testifying before Congress, America's so-called chief infectious disease expert told a House committee that coronavirus was "10 times more lethal than the flu" in testimony that plunged the country into lockdown.[44]

What changed with Fauci in just those eleven days? What new piece of data did he acquire that so dramatically altered his public position on the virus? Could it have been the disgraced Imperial College doomsday model? Perhaps he got an early glimpse, but the model wasn't published until five days later on March 16.[45] So how else can we possibly explain

---

[43] Anthony S. Fauci et al., "Covid-19—Navigating the Uncharted."
[44] "Coronavirus Is 10 Times More Lethal Than Seasonal Flu, Fauci Says," YouTube, March 11, 2020, https://www.youtube.com/watch?v=2DekzGCJhJw.
[45] Neil Ferguson et al., "Report 9: Impact of Non-Pharmaceutical Interventions (NPIs) to Reduce COVID-19 Mortality and Healthcare Demand," Imperial College, March 16, 2020, https://www.imperial.ac.uk/media/imperial-college/medicine/sph/ide/gida-fellowships/Imperial-College-COVID19-NPI-modelling-16-03-2020.pdf.

such a radical about-face from one of our most celebrated "experts"?

Ironically, thanks to largely unreported data from the CDC,[46] Fauci's original measured analysis of the infection fatality rate for coronavirus he predicted in the *New England Journal of Medicine* is looking increasingly prescient. We must learn what happened after he wrote that which caused him to become the pied piper leading America into recession and authoritarianism.

Just as we must also learn why Fauci consistently seems hesitant, at the very least, to respond affirmatively to virtually *any* new positive piece of data. At first, given how unreliable the native data from China likely was, you could forgive Fauci and his ilk for their abundance of caution in the face of an ongoing media onslaught demanding action.

But then our own real-time data began flooding in and hardly jived with the panic porn. By then, though, Fauci was too good at convincing the public lockdowns were the right approach, partially thanks to the feedback loop of the panic the media demanded and his compliance by giving it "expert" consent. The scare was on, and his star was reborn.

---

[46] Daniel Horowitz, "Horowitz: The CDC Confirms Remarkably Low Coronavirus Death Rate. Where Is the Media?" TheBlaze, May 25, 2020, https://www.theblaze.com/op-ed/horowitz-the-cdc-confirms-remarkably-low-coronavirus-death-rate-where-is-the-media.

This is similar to the HIV outbreak of the 1980s, when children in public schools were legit concerned they were gonna get HIV from a toilet seat after Indiana teenager Ryan White contracted it from a blood transfusion.[47] By the way, who was the media's beloved "nation's leading infectious disease expert" during those times? You guessed it, none other than Fauci.[48]

Let's now turn our attention to our second primary question that requires an answer—how do you flatten a curve if you don't know when it began?

Awareness is not an origin date. Gravity existed long before the apple fell on Newton's head. Remember those alarming curve graphs in the early days of the pandemic that showed massive spikes in American coronavirus cases? What was the context? We don't know when the virus truly arrived. So how can we measure the rate of increase to something that lacks a starting point?

We don't have a true patient zero. The earliest documented case of Wuhan flu the United States currently

---

[47] Ryan White HIV/AIDS Program, "Who Was Ryan White," Health Resources & Services Administration, https://hab.hrsa.gov/about-ryan-white-hivaids-program/who-was-ryan-white.

[48] Tim Murphy, "America, Meet Tony Fauci. HIV/AIDS Activists Have Known Him a Long Time," TheBodyPro, March 20, 2020, https://www.thebodypro.com/article/tony-fauci-md-coronavirus.

acknowledges is November 17, 2019.[49] China wouldn't even officially notify the World Health Organization about COVID-19 for almost two more months. There are almost 370,000 Chinese citizens attending college in the US alone,[50] not counting all the other visas we issue from that country. How many of them went home for Christmas or Thanksgiving break during the fourth quarter of 2019 and then brought coronavirus back with them without knowing it because their government lies to them, too?

This isn't like a football game, when there's a mad rush to the concession stand right before and after halftime, therefore if we space out the flow of customers throughout the whole game it puts less strain on the system. We don't even know when halftime is. Nor do we know when the game began, let alone when the parking lots letting in the fans were opened. It is quite possible COVID-19 was here for weeks, if not months, before the public was made aware of its presence.

Patricia Dowd, a fifty-seven-year-old auditor for a Silicon Valley semiconductor manufacturer, died of COVID-19 on

---

[49] Jeanna Bryner, "1st Known Case of Coronavirus Traced Back to November in China," Live Science. March 14, 2020, https://www.livescience.com/first-case-coronavirus-found.html.
[50] "Number of College and University Students from China in the United States from Academic Year 2008/ to 2018/19," Statista, https://www.statista.com/statistics/372900/number-of-chinese-students-that-study-in-the-us/.

February 6, 2020,[51] more than a month before lockdowns began. She remains our earliest specifically recorded coronavirus death. She worked at a company that had an office in Wuhan. Dowd had last visited China in November 2019. Given what we know about the pathology of the virus, she would've been infected sometime well into January at the latest.[52]

On April 20, 2020, with the entire country still mired in the now repackaged "30 days to slow the spread," Southern California University released the findings of its antibody testing of Los Angeles County. Now, keep in mind at this time COVID hot spots were still largely relegated to the East Coast. We hadn't even hit 40,000 US casualties with COVID yet.[53] Most of the country was locked down, waiting for a wave that had yet to arrive despite all the IHME models claiming otherwise.

---

[51] Thomas Fuller et al., "A Coronavirus Death in Early February Was 'Probably the Tip of an Iceberg,'" *New York Times*, April 22, 2020, updated September 14, 2020, https://www.nytimes.com/2020/04/22/us/santa-clara-county-coronavirus-death.html.

[52] Erin Allday and Matthias Gafni, "1st US COVID-19 Death Was 57-Year-Old Santa Clara County Woman, Probe Finds," *San Francisco Chronicle*, April 22, 2020, https://www.sfchronicle.com/bayarea/article/First-U-S-COVID-19-death-was-57-year-old-Santa-15218813.php.

[53] Tucker Reals et al., "Coronavirus Updates from April 16, 2020," CBS News, April 16, 2020, updated April 17, 2020, https://www.cbsnews.com/live-updates/coronavirus-pandemic-covid-19-latest-news-2020-04-16/.

Nevertheless, this antibody study found a surprising 4.1 percent of Los Angeles County residents already showed antibodies from a prior COVID-19 infection, which means anywhere from 28–55 times more people in Los Angeles County already had been infected with coronavirus than the county's official statistics had indicated at the time.[54] Yes, you read that right—**28–55 times more infections** than county health officials had recorded.

As the great Bob Uecker once said, "Just a bit outside." Is it any wonder why so much of our data/models have been so off this entire time with such a flawed baseline to start from? On February 20, 2021, the *Los Angeles Times* marveled at "new optimism that Covid-19 is finally dwindling as L.A. gains some herd immunity."[55] Maybe, just maybe, the reason America's second-largest city "unexpectedly" hit a herd immunity threshold is because from the very beginning their assumptions were off by an order of magnitude?

See, it comes down to this. If the virus was here all along, meaning wreaking havoc most of the flu-pneumonia season before the media/body politic turned this into a full-blown panic, then lockdowns were never going to work. It's like

---

[54] Tucker Reals et al., "Coronavirus Updates."
[55] Soumya Karlamangla and Rong-Gong Lin II, "New Optimism That COVID-19 Is Finally Dwindling as L.A. Gains Some Herd Immunity," *Los Angeles Times*, February 20, 2021, https://www.latimes.com/california/story/2021-02-20/covid-19-pandemic-herd-immunity-vaccinations-plummeting-cases.

closing the barn door after the hay has already left the barn. Applying a condom after consummation. You're too late, what's done is now done. All you can do at this point is identify who has it, who's most vulnerable, and isolate them for protection.

But maybe this wasn't true worldwide? Maybe the size and vastness of the United States, on top of the amount of foreign travel we import/export, meant for us it was too late to lockdown the virus but not elsewhere? No country was more decimated by coronavirus than Italy was. Its first recorded case was February 21, 2020, and it set the nation ablaze shortly thereafter. However, more recent antibody studies indicate infections in the country going all the way back to September 2019.[56]

Knowing the accurate arrival of the coronavirus is a vital component to accurately judge the efficacy of the public policy devised to mitigate its spread. And one thing we likely all agree on, regardless of political preference, is the need for more public policy accountability.

For example, the weeks ending March 7, 2020, and March 14, 2020, were the final two of the 2019–20 flu season before

---

[56] Giselda Vagnoni, "Coronavirus Came to Italy Almost 6 Months Before the First Official Case, New Study Shows," World Economic Forum, November 16, 2020, https://www.weforum.org/agenda/2020/11/coronavirus-italy-covid-19-pandemic-europe-date-antibodies-study.

our entire focus became COVID-19. According to CDC, deaths from flu and pneumonia (CDC classifies them together) were 7.1 percent of all US deaths during that time period, which is just barely below the CDC's epidemic threshold of 7.3 percent.[57] The week ending January 25, 2020, pneumonia and flu deaths were still a robust 7.1 percent of all US mortality, again flirting with the epidemic line.[58]

Is it possible we were seeing patients at that time with similar respiratory issues, but with no way of coding it, yet we were still classifying them as flu and pneumonia? Recall that even now what are common flu and pneumonia symptoms are currently coded as "COVID-like symptoms" when you visit the hospital.

There's no way of knowing, but these are things from a public policy perspective we must know. The doctors and scientists are charged with confronting the virus itself, but in a self-governing constitutional republic it is we the people and our elected representatives who are tasked with how to govern ourselves in light of a pandemic. Prudence requires us to weigh several competing factors to that end, and we cannot do that without accurate data and information.

---

[57] Centers for Disease Control and Prevention, "U.S. Virologic Surveillance," https://www.cdc.gov/flu/weekly/weeklyarchives2019-2020/Week11.htm.
[58] Centers for Disease Control and Prevention, "U.S. Virologic Surveillance," https://www.cdc.gov/flu/weekly/weeklyarchives2019-2020/Week05.htm.

Which is why, once more, a 9/11-style tribunal is required to assess both the origin date of the virus as well as the origin for Fauci's change of heart. We must be prepared for both the next attempt at an authoritarian power grab, as well as the looming possibility we could face a biological threat that legitimately pits our survival against our liberty.

That is not to say the hundreds of thousands of Americans who have tragically died with COVID-19 are a triviality. Quite the contrary, each and every one of those lives were fearfully and wonderfully made—and without question we should mourn with those who mourn.

However, in the context of public policy, the interests of the public as a whole must be weighed and measured. Questions such as "can we protect the most vulnerable while still maintaining our way of life that makes life worth living" are to be answered in this venue. And considering how obvious the data has been about who is and who isn't mortally vulnerable to COVID-19, we believe the answer to that question has been 'yes' for some time now.

Chapter 3

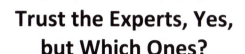

Trust the Experts, Yes, but Which Ones?

From the beginning, the Covidstan media demanded that we "trust the experts." The authors of this book couldn't agree more, but what do you do when not even the experts agree?

Are Yale, Oxford, Stanford, and Carnegie Mellon just some Podunk, renegade community colleges? No, they're obviously some of the most renowned universities on this planet, and their models/analysis paint a different tale than the supposedly infallible Fauci's doomsaying and flip-flops.

Dr. David Katz of Yale, wrote in the noted right-wing/science-denying *New York Times* about his concern our cure (consisting of mass shutdowns) is worse than the disease:

> *I am deeply concerned that the social, economic, and public health consequences of this near total meltdown of normal life—schools and businesses closed, gatherings banned—will be long lasting and calamitous, possibly graver than the direct toll of the*

virus itself. The stock market will bounce back in time, but many businesses never will. The unemployment, impoverishment, and despair likely to result will be public health scourges of the first order. Worse, I fear our efforts will do little to contain the virus, because we have a resource-constrained, fragmented, perennially underfunded public health system. Distributing such limited resources so widely, so shallowly and so haphazardly is a formula for failure. How certain are you of the best ways to protect your most vulnerable loved ones?[59]

Dr. John Ioannidis of Stanford, one of the top five medical schools in the country, penned a peer-reviewed study on the "harms of exaggerated information and non-evidence-based measures" to fight coronavirus. [60] Ioannidis's paper was published March 11, 2020, the very day Fauci gave the doomsday prophecy to Congress that shut down the country. In it, Ioannidis predicted we would see the following: fake news and withdrawn papers, exaggerated pandemic estimates, exaggerated case fatality rates, exaggerated exponential

---

[59] David L. Katz, "Is Our Fight against Coronavirus Worse Than the Disease?" *New York Times*, March 20, 2020, https://www.nytimes.com/2020/03/20/opinion/coronavirus-pandemic-social-distancing.html.

[60] John P. A. Ioannidis, "Coronavirus Disease 2019: The Harms of Exaggerated Information and Non-Evidence-Based Measures," *European Journal of Clinical Investigation* 50, issue 4 (March 19, 2020), https://onlinelibrary.wiley.com/doi/abs/10.1111/eci.13222?casa_token=1kvye2k YQKYAAAAA:ovAGJKRYqXa3DojbZ2oYjZ3h8jBKXq5RiVfmIOUSadKWn eW8lZgbAWhBCViNs4WDTE25Q2O9c6XVTyrR.

community spread, extreme measures, harms from non-evidenced based measures, misallocation of resources, lockdowns, economic and social disruption, claims of a once-in-a-century pandemic, and comparisons to the 1918 Spanish flu. He was sadly prophetic with every claim.

Sunetra Gupta is a professor of theoretical epidemiology at venerable Oxford, the top-ranked university in the world, and she directly contradicted the discredited apocalyptic Imperial College simulation that spooked our own government into starting the lockdowns.[61]

Wesley Pegden is an associate professor of mathematics at Carnegie Mellon, one of the leading research universities in the country, and he pointed out the data simulations demanding indefinite mass shutdowns/social-distancing had a poison pill:

> *The duration of containment does not matter. As long as a large majority of the population remains uninfected, lifting containment measures will lead to an epidemic almost as large as would happen without having mitigations in place.*[62]

---

[61] Clive Cookson, "Coronavirus May Have Infected Half of UK Population—Oxford Study," *Financial Times*, March 24, 2020, https://www.ft.com/content/5ff6469a-6dd8-11ea-89df-41bea055720b.
[62] James Barrett, "Professors Push Back on Pandemic Models: Be Honest about What Happens after Lockdowns Are Lifted," Daily Wire, March 31, 2020,

We have seen Pegden's point confirmed in countries like New Zealand, Australia, Israel, and the United Kingdom—each of which have done multiple waves of lockdowns. Because without natural or vaccination immunity, if a zero-tolerance policy for cases regardless of lethality is your goal, you're never really out of lockdown. You're just in-between lockdowns.

One of the most famous infectious disease experts used the occasion of the far more lethal Ebola virus to make his case against "draconian" lockdowns. This despite the fact the average case fatality rate for Ebola, according to the World Health Organization, is a monstrous 50 percent—which is 2,173 percent more deadly than COVID-19.[63] This famous infectious disease expert had this to say about governors in both major political parties issuing quarantines for travel to Africa, even for health care workers, to combat the cataclysmic Ebola virus back in 2014:

> *Go with science. The best way to stop this epidemic is to help the people in West Africa. We do that by sending people over there (not locking Africa away from the world). We need to treat them, returning*

---

https://www.dailywire.com/news/professors-push-back-on-pandemic-models-be-honest-about-what-happens-after-lockdowns-are-lifted?fbclid=IwAR1NDvlivkPo9FCDKVLQvqAUqcq6SxKSSlU0bLxj2iyAjFo5lhNWsUB0FZg.

[63] World Health Organization, "Ebola Virus Disease," https://www.who.int/health-topics/ebola/#tab=tab_1.

> *people (back home) with respect...(those healthcare*
> *workers) are really our heroes, so the idea we're being*
> *a little bit draconian (via quarantines), there are other*
> *ways to protect (against them bringing Ebola with*
> *them back here).*[64]

For the record, would you like to know the name of this famous infectious disease expert opposed to locking down Africa from the rest of the world, and quarantining our health care workers, against a cosmically more deadly contagion?

His name was none other than Anthony Fauci.

Then there's the curious case of hydroxychloroquine, or the drug Fauci and the Covidstan media openly and obsessively rooted against throughout the early months of the pandemic. Almost as if they didn't want a cure/treatment early on, or at the very least not one that didn't require billions of dollars in new grants for cutting-edge big pharma.

The authors of this book don't know what to think about hydroxychloroquine's effectiveness in treating COVID-19, precisely because we're not doctors or scientists. We also have seen contradictory studies on the matter, including one of the most-celebrated critiques of the drug from the medical journal *The Lancet*—which was later retracted for "potential flaws in

---

[64] Michael Ruiz, "Fauci Warned of 'Unintended Consequences' of 'Draconian' Quarantines during 2014 Ebola Outbreak," Fox News, February 19, 2021, https://www.foxnews.com/us/dr-fauci-quarantines-2014-ebola-outbreak.

the resource data."[65] Dr. Daniel Culver of the Cleveland Clinic told NBC News the study was so flawed "a first-year statistics major could tell you about major flaws in the design of the analysis."

However, just over a month after the retraction of *The Lancet* study, which was the most exhaustive one yet on hydroxychloroquine and coronavirus, Fauci spoke out definitively against the drug:

> *You look at the scientific data and the evidence. And the scientific data on trials that are valid, that were randomized and controlled in the proper way, all of those trials show consistently that hydroxychloroquine is not effective in the treatment of coronavirus disease or Covid-19.*[66]

We wouldn't presume to debate Dr. Fauci on a topic he knows much more about than we do. But what about experts at schools 99.99 percent of this world couldn't get into? Are they permitted to tug on Superman's cape?

---

[65] Erika Edwards, "*The Lancet* Retracts Large Study on Hydroxychloroquine," NBC News, June 4, 2020, https://www.nbcnews.com/health/health-news/lancet-retracts-large-study-hydroxychloroquine-n1225091.

[66] Berkeley Lovelace Jr., "Dr. Fauci Says All the 'Valid' Scientific Data Shows Hydroxychloroquine Isn't Effective in Treating Coronavirus," CNBC, https://www.cnbc.com/2020/07/29/dr-fauci-says-all-the-valid-scientific-data-shows-hydroxychloroquine-isnt-effective-in-treating-coronavirus.html.

Shortly after Fauci's all but declaring hydroxychloroquine an urban legend, Dr. Harvey Risch of Yale's school of public health called the drug "the key to defeating COVID-19" in an op-ed he wrote for *Newsweek*:

> *On May 27, I published an article in the* American Journal of Epidemiology *(AJE) entitled, "Early Outpatient Treatment of Symptomatic, High-Risk COVID-19 Patients that Should be Ramped-Up Immediately as Key to the Pandemic Crisis." That article, published in the world's leading epidemiology journal, analyzed five studies, demonstrating clear-cut and significant benefits to treated patients, plus other very large studies that showed the medication safety. Physicians who have been using these medications in the face of widespread skepticism have been truly heroic. They have done what the science shows is best for their patients, often at great personal risk. I myself know of two doctors who have saved the lives of hundreds of patients with these medications, but are now fighting state medical boards to save their licenses and reputations. The cases against them are completely without scientific merit. Since publication of my May 27 article, seven more studies have demonstrated similar benefit. A reverse natural experiment happened in Switzerland. On May 27, the Swiss national government banned outpatient*

use of hydroxychloroquine for COVID-19. Around June 10, COVID-19 deaths increased four-fold and remained elevated. On June 11, the Swiss government revoked the ban, and on June 23 the death rate reverted to what it had been beforehand.[67]

We're not experts on hydroxychloroquine, but as hosts of a daily news talk show on one of the largest platforms in the country, we are experts on irreconcilable narratives. Somebody is wrong and/or lying here—Fauci or Risch—because what each of them are asserting the data says about the efficacy of hydroxychloroquine directly contradicts the other. Risch, by the way, is the author of over 330 original peer-reviewed research publications whose work has been cited more than 40,000 times. But if you dare defy Fauci and/or Covidstan, you're suddenly a quack, we guess.

Risch also received backup from Dr. Stephen Smith of the Center for Infectious Diseases. Smith, a Duke and Yale grad who did his post-doctorate training at the National Institutes of Allergies and Infectious Diseases, also called hydroxychloroquine a "game-changer" on national television

---

[67] Harvey A. Risch, "The Key to Defeating COVID-19 Already Exists. We Need to Start Using It," *Newsweek*, July 23, 2020, https://www.newsweek.com/key-defeating-covid-19-already-exists-we-need-start-using-it-opinion-1519535.

before the full brunt of the offensive from Covidstan to shun the drug began.[68]

Perhaps *The American Journal of Medicine* rendered the definitive verdict on this debate with its published paper on January 21, 2021, in which it recommended it was "prudent to deploy" hydroxychloroquine alongside azithromycin and zinc "with the aim of reducing hospitalization and death."[69]

As of the time this book was being written, Fauci had yet to amend his past public criticism of hydroxychloroquine in light of this scientific update. It is entirely possible that this drug does work and lives were lost because it was politicized for various reasons—none of them good—early on in the pandemic. This is the danger, again, of vesting so much power in the hands of one man who is unaccountable to the will of the people, rather than seeking wisdom in a multitude of counsel. From the beginning, there has been ample and robust scientific/academic debate over coronavirus, its potential treatments, and mitigation strategies. Unfortunately, for reasons only he and God know, Fauci has repeatedly opted

---

[68] Nickie Louise, "'Hydroxychloroquine Is a Game Changer and the Beginning of the End Coronavirus Pandemic,' Infectious Disease Specialist Dr. Stephen Smith Says," Tech Startups, April 1, 2020, https://techstartups.com/2020/04/01/hydroxychloroquine-game-changer-beginning-end-coronavirus-pandemic-infectious-disease-specialist-dr-stephen-smith-says/?fbclid=IwAR0VUHUEkuN-pNC43OZJg22c2hbjY95VDhlWCDVirk0pE9WkTa_kb21G1Rk.
[69] Peter A. McCullough et al., "Pathophysiological Basis and Rationale."

against scientific inquiry in exchange for ruthlessly pursuing one particular narrative.

Why aren't these counter-experts' opinions as valid? Why have we not seen these differing opinions vet each other? How come they're never asked about at White House press briefings with Fauci, who is obviously the biggest influence on American policy at the moment? Is Fauci even considering these counter-experts, before recommending that presidents pursue a draconian public policy that led to a higher unemployment rate than the second year of the Great Depression? Wouldn't you like to know the answers to these questions? Don't you think we deserve to know them? Because it will be people like us, not the bureaucrats, who will be left to pick up the pieces of what's left of our economy and way of life when this is over.

Experts have expertise you and I don't have, but they're not necessarily wiser, nor are they any less sinful. Experts are also wrong all the time, because they're human, too.

Experts told Admiral Nimitz he was dumb to listen to one Japanese code-breaker and risk much of our remaining Naval fleet on an ambush at Midway, which ended up turning the tide of the Pacific theater in World War II. Experts told the apostles there's no such thing as a resurrection. Experts differed mightily with Copernicus and Galileo. We could go on and on.

Plenty of "experts" right now think there are fifty-seven genders, and human life happened because two amino acids formed a single-celled protein 600 million years ago for no reason whatsoever. Plenty of "experts" also love them some of those open borders that allowed China to export its Wuhan virus to our shores. Beware of easily handing your sovereignty over to the experts, especially without skeptical vetting. For sure, experts have done amazing things for humanity as well. But a critical time such as this requires more questions, not fewer.

Accountability never made any of us worse. But a lack of it sure does.

Toward the end of his administration, it became obvious President Trump had finally had it with Fauci's antics and exploits. Trump invited Dr. Scott Atlas from Stanford University to join the Coronavirus Task Force, and Atlas took center stage in trying to reset the narrative. We asked Atlas if he could quantify for us the cost of not seeking wisdom in a multitude of counsel. Of not pitting the best and brightest minds against each other in a zealous pursuit of the truth, no matter what, and instead investing all this power in the hands of one unelected bureaucrat whose will mostly goes unchallenged. Atlas replied:

This has gone on so long that people have lost track of why the original shutdowns were done in the early stages of the pandemic. In the beginning no one was prepared for a potential case fatality rate of 3.4%, so a short-term shutdown was appropriate to flatten the curve to stop hospitals from being overcrowded so other medical care could go on. It was also appropriate to buy time for the ramping up and procuring of equipment. Though it was rare, there were some hospitals that were overcrowded.

But after the short-term shutdown it got out of hand. Its purpose was not to stop all cases, which isn't a realistic goal. When you do a lockdown as we have seen all over the world, you do not eliminate the virus. All you do is delay the infection. Then we're testing asymptomatic people who are in the workforce, and shutting down low risk environments like schools. When you do that, all you are going to do is have these cases come later in the winter. And in the winter you do not have the ability to use social distance, eat outdoors, etc. We're locking people down in their homes, and the most frequent place where cases are spread are in the home.[70]

Atlas then ran down a potentially tragic list of unintended consequences.

---

[70] "Dr. Scott Atlas UNLOADS on Lockdowns, Fake Science," *Steve Deace Show*, YouTube, October 20, 2020, https://www.youtube.com/watch?v=QPuEU3I5_YI.

> *The lockdown was a heinous abuse of government and misguided policy. 46% of the six most common cancers were not diagnosed. 85% of living organ donor transplants were not done. Two-thirds of cancer screenings were not done. Half of the 650,000 people on chemotherapy did not come in for chemo. Half of our immunizations didn't get done. The United Nations says 1.3 million will die from starvation because we were shut down and couldn't get them food. More than 200,000 cases of child abuse went unreported. 400,000 more will die from tuberculosis because of a diversion of those resources.*[71]

When, if ever, have you heard Fauci wrestling with the tradeoff of coronavirus lockdowns? When, if ever, have you ever seen him challenged on these grounds?

As we noted at the end of the previous chapter, we should mourn for all the lives taken by COVID-19. But where is the mourning for the lives that will be lost from other lethal maladies, as noted by Atlas? Experts are now also warning of a looming "mental health pandemic" among our young people.[72]

---

[71] "Dr. Scott Atlas UNLOADS," YouTube.

[72] Isabella Kwai and Elian Peltier, "'What's the Point?' Young People's Despair Deepens as Covid-19 Crisis Drags On," *New York Times*, February 14, 2021, updated February 16, 2021, https://www.nytimes.com/2021/02/14/world/europe/youth-mental-health-covid.html.

Mental Health America is reporting an astounding 93 percent increase in anxiety screenings in the past year.[73]

On October 4, 2020, forty-four global experts, representing some of the leading universities in the world, came together to issue "The Great Barrington Declaration." It reads as follows:

> *As infectious disease epidemiologists and public health scientists we have grave concerns about the damaging physical and mental health impacts of the prevailing COVID-19 policies, and recommend an approach we call Focused Protection.*
>
> *Coming from both the left and right, and around the world, we have devoted our careers to protecting people. Current lockdown policies are producing devastating effects on short and long-term public health. The results (to name a few) include lower childhood vaccination rates, worsening cardiovascular disease outcomes, fewer cancer screenings and deteriorating mental health—leading to greater excess mortality in years to come, with the working class and younger members of society carrying the heaviest*

---

[73] Kieran Nicholson, "Mental Health Screenings and Studies Show Big Jumps in Anxiety, Depression during the Pandemic," *Denver Post*, February 18, 2021, https://www.denverpost.com/2021/02/18/mental-health-colorado-pandemic-anxiety-depression/.

burden. Keeping students out of school is a grave injustice.

Keeping these measures in place until a vaccine is available will cause irreparable damage, with the underprivileged disproportionately harmed.

Fortunately, our understanding of the virus is growing. We know that vulnerability to death from COVID-19 is more than a thousand-fold higher in the old and infirm than the young. Indeed, for children, COVID-19 is less dangerous than many other harms, including influenza.

As immunity builds in the population, the risk of infection to all—including the vulnerable—falls. We know that all populations will eventually reach herd immunity—i.e. the point at which the rate of new infections is stable—and that this can be assisted by (but is not dependent upon) a vaccine. Our goal should therefore be to minimize mortality and social harm until we reach herd immunity.

The most compassionate approach that balances the risks and benefits of reaching herd immunity, is to allow those who are at minimal risk of death to live their lives normally to build up immunity to the virus through natural infection, while better protecting those who are at highest risk. We call this Focused Protection.

Adopting measures to protect the vulnerable should be the central aim of public health responses to COVID-19. By way of example, nursing homes should use staff with acquired immunity and perform frequent testing of other staff and all visitors. Staff rotation should be minimized. Retired people living at home should have groceries and other essentials delivered to their home. When possible, they should meet family members outside rather than inside. A comprehensive and detailed list of measures, including approaches to multi-generational households, can be implemented, and is well within the scope and capability of public health professionals.

Those who are not vulnerable should immediately be allowed to resume life as normal. Simple hygiene measures, such as hand washing and staying home when sick should be practiced by everyone to reduce the herd immunity threshold. Schools and universities should be open for in-person teaching. Extracurricular activities, such as sports, should be resumed. Young low-risk adults should work normally, rather than from home. Restaurants and other businesses should open. Arts, music, sports, and other cultural activities should resume. People who are more at risk may participate if they wish, while society as a whole enjoys the

> *protection conferred upon the vulnerable by those who*
> *have built up herd immunity.[74]*

Once again, the authors of this book do not even pretend to be qualified to determine whether or not the experts who issued this declaration are more precise in their analysis of COVID-19 than is Fauci. However, we do believe the American people are constitutionally qualified to benefit from such a debate. We got brief glimpses of how Fauci behaves when challenged not once,[75] but twice,[76] by Senator Rand Paul, who is also a doctor (and who also contracted coronavirus early on). After participating in numerous debates over the years, we've always viewed the type of defensiveness displayed by Fauci at even surface-level pushback as being indicative of a weak argument that lacks substantive answers for its grandiose claims.

Still, let us not become guilty of the very same magical thinking and projection we've too often seen from Covidstan. Just because the narrative of those who signed "The Great Barrington Declaration" is calling for a more preferable way of

---

[74] Martin Kulldorff et al., "The Great Barrington Declaration," October 4, 2020, https://gbdeclaration.org/.

[75] "Sen. Rand Paul Challenges Dr. Fauci. Watch His Response." YouTube, June 30, 2020, https://www.youtube.com/watch?v=ZYk3T39Xa4Y.

[76] "Exchange between Sen. Rand Paul and Dr. Anthony Fauci," YouTube, May 12, 2020, https://www.youtube.com/watch?v=D5wSe4w9Tv4.

life than lockdowns doesn't mean they're right. But don't we deserve to know what the truth is, either way?

Furthermore, whatever happened to a skeptical media? How come the media ignores, disregards, or humiliates anyone who dares defy Fauci's view of things?

Chapter 4

President Fauci

Donald Trump's reelection prospects looked a lot more promising in the pre-coronavirus world.

On February 17, 2020, almost exactly one month to the day before the United States launched "15 days to flatten the election year economy curve," FoxBusiness.com ran a lengthy profile of the economy under President Trump's leadership. It included the following information:

> *The stock market grew 31% in the 807 trading days before Trump's election, but it grew by 56% in the 807 trading days after it.... Manufacturing rose 3.6% during Trump's three years, which was more than double the rise of 1.7% in the first three years under Obama...487,000 manufacturing jobs were created...the Congressional Budget Office forecast the creation of only two million jobs (under Trump), the economy has actually created seven million jobs.... Nominal wages for the lowest 10% of American*

> *workers jumped 7%, the (wage) growth rate for those*
> *without a high school diploma was 9%.*[77]

In other words, both those at the top (stock market gains) and those coming up from the bottom (wages for those without a high school diploma) were benefitting from the Trump presidency. But what about the middle class? Economist Stephen Moore of The Heritage Foundation, writing for The Hill in January 2020, had this to say:

> *Incomes are up at least $4,000 per household for the middle class, adjusted for inflation under Trump. That compares with $1,000 per household gain in incomes under Obama over eight years.... Overall median household family incomes have risen by almost 8% in just three years under Trump, compared to almost no gains throughout the previous 16 years.*[78]

Even the anti-Trump *Washington Post* ran a headline admitting, "Americans say they feel like this is the best economy since the late 1990s"[79] on February 10, 2021,

---

[77] Maxim Lott, "The Trump Economy, Three Years In: What the Numbers Say," Fox Business, February 17, 2020, https://www.foxbusiness.com/markets/trump-economy-three-years-in.

[78] Stephen Moore, "Contrary to What the Media Reports, Middle Class Americans Are Surging," The Hill, January 6, 2020, https://thehill.com/opinion/finance/476959-contrary-to-what-the-media-reports-middle-class-americans-are-surging.

[79] Heather Long, "Americans Say They Feel Like This Is the Best Economy Since the Late 1990s," *Washington Post*, February 10. 2020,

including a subhead noting the "surge in confidence." In the fall of 2019, CNBC highlighted "Black and Hispanic unemployment is at a record low."[80] And according to the Trump White House, his administration could also claim credit for the following amid a lengthy list of accomplishments:

> *Lifted nearly seven million off of food stamps.... Unemployment for women hit its lowest rate in nearly 70 years.... Income inequality fell two straight years, and by the largest amount in over a decade.... Home prices hit an all-time high.*[81]

Let's be honest, this is not typically the record of a one-term president. And it likely wouldn't have been had there never been a COVID-19, especially given the fact the controversies that surrounded the mail-in aspect of the 2020 election would've likely never occurred. Without COVID-19, we would've proceeded with mostly in-person voting as we

---

https://www.washingtonpost.com/business/2020/02/10/americans-feel-good-economy/.

[80] Maggie Fitzgerald, "Black and Hispanic Unemployment Is at a Record Low," CNBC, October 4, 2019, https://www.cnbc.com/2019/10/04/black-and-hispanic-unemployment-is-at-a-record-low.html.

[81] "Trump Administration Accomplishments, as of January 2021," Trump White House Archives, https://trumpwhitehouse.archives.gov/trump-administration-accomplishments/.

always have, with at least thirty-five states enforcing voter ID laws.[82]

Trump, and really all political leaders regardless of ideological persuasion, can probably be forgiven for the initial wave of lockdowns. We couldn't trust the virus data we were getting from China. Both the media and the public were in an unprecedented uproar. You couldn't buy toilet paper, in America of all places, in the twenty-first century. Those were scary times for most of us. Erring heavily on the side of caution can hardly be considered an unforgivable sin.

However, when "15 days to flatten the curve" became "30 days to slow the spread," that's when the dumbest management decision in American history was cemented and Trump effectively handed over the reins of his presidency to Anthony Fauci indefinitely. For all intents and purposes, in the minds of much of America, Fauci was now president. He had become the most powerful bureaucrat in American history. The Trump White House lost the narrative on the virus/lockdowns/reopening/normalcy for good, or at least until the president himself left the hospital with renewed vigor and optimism after recovering from COVID-19 in the final weeks of the 2020 campaign. But by then the die had been cast.

---

[82] "Voter Identification Requirements—Voter ID Laws," National Conference of State Legislatures, August 25, 2020, https://www.ncsl.org/research/elections-and-campaigns/voter-id.aspx.

Leaders make mistakes. Even the great ones. But what makes them great is learning from the mistakes that have already been made. Rather than repeating them, or doubling-down on them.

The combination of the death/socioeconomic toll has made coronavirus by far the worst domestic calamity in our nation since the Civil War. And we've probably not been more divided/polarized as a people since that era, either.

In the nascent months of the Civil War, General George B. McClellan looked like a capable commanding general. He won some early battles and prepped the Union Army for the war. But as the Civil War entered its second year, it became more and more obvious that once the Confederate enemy evolved he could not do the same.

Union morale and confidence sank as a result. McClellan also found President Abraham Lincoln to be beneath him when it came to expertise and loathed taking military advice from a politician. This often made him slow to act against a fast-moving enemy, and put the Union behind the curve.

We have reset this historical anecdote because this should sound familiar. After Antietam, the bloodiest battle in US history, Lincoln had finally had enough. McClellan failed to pursue Robert E. Lee, leader of the Confederate forces, and allowed him to escape to potentially prolong the war. Lincoln finally made the move he probably should've already made long before and fired McClellan.

We, the authors of this book, believe the main reason Trump was not reelected is he never made the decision he should've made—firing Fauci—once it became clear Fauci was behind the curve he was allegedly trying to flatten. Lincoln was late in firing McClellan, but thankfully it wasn't too late to hire his Ulysses S. Grant. Together they won the Civil War and preserved the Union. Yet Trump is now out of office while Fauci remains.

Whether it's all the different opinions Fauci continues to give on COVID-19, ranging from a Frank Drebin "nothing to see here" to a Denathorian "run for your lives." His slavish devotion to models he later said he didn't trust. All the doublespeak and new speak. His pesky penchant for ignoring/diminishing anything that even teases optimism. His denial of the basic laws/precedents of science, virology, and immunology. His McClellanesque antics of undermining the president he worked for.

It was clear by the summer of 2020 that Fauci either didn't know what he was talking about, was making it up as he went along, was really bad at this, just wasn't capable of being intellectually honest, or was a willing/unwilling participant in an election year black op (or a mixture of several, if not all, the options here).

At the very least, somewhere along the line Fauci forgot we are not his patients; we are the people, and this is a government by and for the people. Not by and for a swamp of unelected bureaucrats, who last so long in government they become its highest-paid employee.[83]

For most of this pandemic, the American people have been offered a false choice between either pretending this was just a bad flu so nothing should be done, or hiding out in your homes until the vaccines arrive. And at the time this book was being written, that false choice had morphed into 'the vaccines are here but we still need lockdowns and double masks.'

But there always was a third way.

How did previous generations industrialize America and win two world wars despite the far more vicious polio virus? Even during the Spanish flu epidemic a century ago, they still played sporting events with fans in the stands. Yet for the better part of 2020, your kids couldn't be in school or you couldn't visit a dentist in much of America.

What changed is those previous generations understood they were not masters of their own fate. That their rights came

---

[83] Adam Andrzejewski, "Dr. Anthony Fauci: The Highest Paid Employee in the Entire U.S. Federal Government," *Forbes*, January 25, 2021, https://www.forbes.com/sites/adamandrzejewski/2021/01/25/dr-anthony-fauci-the-highest-paid-employee-in-the-entire-us-federal-government/?sh=1c269ef3386f.

from God, as did their lives. That there is also evil at work in the world and all creation groans with sin, which is why we have vicious viral outbreaks in the first place. That humanity is more than a survival rate. That the greatest story ever told was about a life that only lasted thirty-three years.

We have either lost sight of, or betrayed, those fundamentals of our existence and that cultural heritage. We have made the perfect the enemy of the good by seeking first to avoid any suffering in life, rather than accept it is our lot to suffer at times while journeying east of Eden, and therefore our generational charge is to do our best with the time we have to pass on the American Dream.

One worldview inspires Americans to protect the vulnerable at the same time we prize our liberties and maintain our rights. The other worldview tells us all to settle in for some Netflix and chill. Besides, who needs a Gettysburg Address when you've got *Tiger King* to binge-watch?

In September 2020, the anti-Trump media was ecstatic about the release of Bob Woodward's new book *Rage*, which claimed Trump told its author he purposely (and falsely) diminished the severity of coronavirus "to avoid panic."[84]

---

[84] "Bob Woodward Book *Rage*: Trump Denies Lying about Risks of Coronavirus," BBC News, September 10, 2020, https://www.bbc.com/news/world-us-canada-54107677.

Except what the media was unintentionally admitting is this was really the trial of President Fauci, not President Trump.

The math goes something like this. Trump knew it was bad but told the public everything would be OK. Then he simply watched as millions died because of his willful deceit against both science and compassion.

Well, math is hard for some, and this mental math doesn't check out at all.

Trump shut down travel from China (good), then locked down the economy he had previously reinvigorated to the tune of historically catastrophic unemployment levels (bad). Meanwhile, deaths per capita across the country largely fell into a grouping of worldwide and flu-on-steroids norms, which occurred almost no matter what interventions were taken (perhaps you've heard of Sweden, more on that later).

And that's if you can believe the data about what actually counts as a coronavirus death, which you probably can't.[85] And yes, we know this wasn't Trump's finest hour by a long shot. Here's the kicker, though: Fauci was at Trump's side for it all.

---

[85] Dave Bondy, "CDC: 94% of Covid-19 Deaths Had Underlying Medical Conditions," NBC 25 News, August 30, 2020, https://nbc25news.com/news/local/cdc-94-of-covid-19-deaths-had-underlying-medical-conditions.

You can think anything you want about the efficacy or sound-mindedness of how Trump played things out, but what you can't do is pretend that Fauci didn't have a hand in it—or even likely guided it. That's the same Fauci the media has canonized with a cult-like devotion (more on that later, too). They made Fauci infallible. We had to trust him, no matter how many times he was wrong about everything all the time. He was going to save us from Trump killing us all.

Of course, the reality is the exact opposite—as it usually is when it comes to our media. The reality is the worst thing Trump did his entire presidency is entrust it to Fauci the fraud. His heinous lockdowns did untold damage to this country that will take years and years to dig out from.

Just where did Trump get the notion that COVID-19 would just be a bad flu, one of the media's most oft-reset criticisms of the former president? Why, from Fauci himself, who wrote those very words in the illustrious *New England Journal of Medicine* back on February 28, 2020.[86]

See, when it comes to having red in the ledger, Trump was more accomplice than point man on multiple fronts. That's on him, yes, but accomplices need perpetrators to enable. That makes Trump's grave sin submitting to the

---

[86] Anthony S. Fauci et al., "Covid-19—Navigating the Uncharted."

"expertise" of Fauci, who has proven to be an expert at nothing other than building his own brand.

Fauci's designs for America over the course of 2020's virus-palooza ran the gamut from "nothing to see here" to "maybe you better put your goggles on." From "rub some dirt on it" to "death comes to us all." And it doesn't really matter if he had held these varied positions because he was legitimately following what he believed to be true, is utterly incompetent, or is a debased liar. The end results are the same nevertheless.

Believe "the experts" we were and still are told to this very day with Karen-filled scorn. And Trump, much to our chagrin, repeatedly did. Or at least Fauci-variety experts, until it was too late. That's where you can place his guilt if there is any to be found. Their scalps are in this together. Trump may have held the title president, but Fauci has been the emperor. So scream that the emperor has no clothes all you want, but no one's bare bottom is more exposed than "in Fauci we trust."

In April 2020, while still mired in "30 days to slow the spread" lockdowns, we published the following brief essay on the Facebook page for our show:

> *Small businesses, like ours that owns our show, make up over 40% of the U.S. economy. So while it's great we can still go to Target and Walmart, many of these are businesses that simply cannot just pause and then restart like nothing happened. Even with the loan*

program now in place. Also consider, the clear majority of new jobs created each year in our economy come from small–midsized businesses. So you're not simply going to get this going again by all the major corporations adding 10k–100k new jobs. Not when there's already 17 million unemployment claims now (not counting those who have yet to file, or the backlog of filings) and climbing. Finally, consider 90%+ of American companies before this began had 500 or fewer employees. And that's after three straight solid years of growth from 2017–19.

Translation: this just cannot go on another 4–8 weeks like White House economic adviser Larry Kudlow said yesterday. The models are garbage. The apocalypse this ain't. The cost to our way of life simply isn't justified.

And then there's the petty tyrants in our political class, who will continue to get grosser to justify their newfound authority the more obvious it becomes the models they used to power-grab are garbage. Because that's how government works. It never volunteers deference or humility. Such qualities must be demanded. A government by the consent of the governed.

Government is only force, and it is only a force for good when the people make it so. Similar to a fire, but a fire left on its own will set everything ablaze. It needs to be controlled and maintained.

Trump defied all the conventional wisdom to become president because he became a populist voice for the forgotten American. It is time for those forgotten Americans to rise up, remind him you're his base, and demand/encourage he take back the presidency you elected him to from the likes of Fauci.

For when this drags on for too long, and the unemployment claims rise along with the tyranny, it won't be Fauci who is vulnerable to a voter backlash but Trump.[87]

Unfortunately, it would be many months later before Trump would attempt to marginalize Fauci and recover his presidency from Fauci's clutches. Too many months later, that is. By then, the damage was done. Everything we warned about in this April essay had been fulfilled, and then some. Too much of it is still taking place even now, at the time this book was being written. Fauci has gone from telling us not to wear masks to telling us to wear two of them, just to be on the safe side. He was also undermining the very vaccines he told us to wait for, which drew the ire of Ben Shapiro:

---

[87] Steve Deace, Facebook, April 9, 2020, https://www.facebook.com/stevedeace/photos/small-businesses-like-mine-that-owns-our-show-make-up-over-40-of-the-us-economy-/1475234302656604/.

> *Fauci should be fired. He has been down-talking the efficacy of vaccines at a time when we need precisely the opposite. He has been mirroring [Biden's] double-talk on school re-openings. I gave Fauci the benefit of the doubt for a full year here, but he is simply not an apolitical voice at this point.*[88]

Fauci even had the unmitigated gall to shamelessly say the "U.S. response to coronavirus is among the worst in the world."[89] That's the very response he was, and still is, in charge of.

Fauci seemingly remains as ascendant as ever, while Trump has left office and been silenced from social media.

You will either drain the swamp, or it will drain you.

---

[88] Ben Shapiro (@benshapiro), Twitter, February 22, 2021, https://twitter.com/benshapiro/status/1363843521501888519.
[89] Graig Graziosi, "Dr. Fauci Says US Response to Coronavirus among the Worst in the World," *Independent*, February 22, 2021, https://www.independent.co.uk/news/world/americas/us-politics/dr-fauci-us-response-coronavirus-b1805892.html.

Chapter 5

An Interview with Veritas

Every truth movement requires whistleblower(s). Someone, or several someones, who can pierce the veil of the dysfunction and deception we believe we can circumstantially prove, or instinctively sense is there, but without such eyewitness testimony we're left to little more than dot-connecting. Attempting to make sense of the senseless, we can't help but be guilty of projection to some extent without our whistleblower(s).

Thankfully, this book has ours.

Just as the legendary (or infamous) "deep throat" was the Rosetta Stone of Watergate,[90] we have our own guide(s) through the killing fields of truth and clarity presided over by Fauci. Their name is *Veritas*.

---

[90] Annette McDermott, "How 'Deep Throat' Took Down Nixon from Inside the FBI," History, September 27, 2018, https://www.history.com/news/watergate-deep-throat-fbi-informant-nixon.

Veritas could be one person, could be several. They may be male or female. But let's face it, in the realm of politicized junk science that is Fauci's natural habitat, transcendent existential fundamentals such as gender just aren't that relevant anymore. In this worldview, science isn't truth discovered but outcome conjured. We just decide which outcome we want and then call whatever hellish process it takes to get there "science."

Those such as our *Veritas* disdain this subjectivism repackaged as "science" with every fiber of their being, which is why they spoke to us. On the condition of anonymity, we conducted this composite Q&A to get the unvarnished view from inside the Trump White House. *Veritas* held nothing back, but be forewarned. What you're about to read will not satisfy you.

What did you know about Anthony Fauci before COVID-19?

VERITAS: Nothing other than his title and his reputation. He wasn't really involved in policy or the administration at all before coronavirus.

Can you describe the evolution of Fauci's influence and power, and how you saw it evolve and accumulate?

VERITAS: Early on it seemed the team of "medical experts" were pretty equal in clout. Debbie Birx had as much influence as Fauci. CDC Director Michael Redfield had as much say as Birx, and so on. But since this entire team came from largely the same gene pool, if you will, Birx and Fauci started to move forward. Because that's what they do, and they came in highly-regarded for their past work on infectious diseases, global pandemics, and their work on AIDS. However, as time went on and we started getting real-time data beyond just these frightening models and projections, that data didn't always corroborate the narrative. So we began to push back on them, and not always because we disagreed or suspected something was amiss, but because science is by definition supposed to be tested not just taken at face value because someone said so. Fauci would not always take well to that, and when you're having these conversations internally eventually you're going to defer to doctors you presume have more knowledge of such airborne viruses. But their stories didn't always add up. For example, we were originally told there was no human-to-human transmission. Obviously, that didn't turn out to be true. There were other things that didn't turn out to be true, too, but it's a novel virus so at first you want/need to trust your experts to some degree. Especially when you've got airports and cruise ships still out there that could be mass carrier events, and you're struggling to get a handle on the situation as soon as you can. And it was Fauci who said repeatedly, not just in the news but also in meetings, that the flu was much worse. He even told us at first that Covid wasn't something we should be concerned about, and that we don't need masks.

Didn't Fauci later admit he lied about not needing to wear masks to prevent a run-on masks?

VERITAS: Yes, but it wasn't just that. Fauci also told us privately within the White House we didn't need to wear masks. I think that's something most people don't understand. The president wasn't making stuff up. He was hearing things from our experts, especially Fauci, and then saying exactly what they were telling him. Originally he trusted Fauci completely. One of the first times Fauci came to the press room he was asked by reporters if they could take their vacations, because that's all they seemed to care about. And he told them, sure, unless you're not feeling well if you want to take a cruise that's fine, you won't need masks, and the flu is much worse. That's also what he was telling our people within the White House. But then, all of a sudden, when coronavirus began showing up in other states and spreading, he just changed his tune out of the blue. He had no studies to point to, and started telling us we were gonna have to wear masks, when he previously pointed to studies that showed wearing masks could even make an outbreak worse because we're constantly touching and therefore tainting the mask or at least rendering it ineffective. He told the White House the average person doesn't know how to properly wear a mask, which is true, and there's even classes in med school where professionals are taught proper usage. However, literally out of nowhere he changed with no explanation.

On February 28, 2020, Fauci wrote a piece in the New England Journal of Medicine comparing the case fatality rate for COVID-19 with the flu. He even described the CFR for COVID-19 as "akin to those of a severe seasonal influenza (which has a case fatality rate of approximately 0.1%) or a pandemic influenza."[91] In this piece, in perhaps the nation's most-respected medical journal, he was making this direct comparison. He was making the direct comparison. Eleven days later he went to Congress and testified that this was going to kill ten times more people than the flu.[92] That was the testimony that essentially shut America down. One of the great unsolved mysteries of this story is what did Fauci learn between February 28 and March 11 that so dramatically changed his tune? Was there some data he shared with the White House that convinced him this had gone from a bad flu to a cataclysmic event during that time?

VERITAS: As was alluded to before, inside the White House they also saw a sudden and inexplicable change from Fauci right around that time as well. No new evidence or data was shared to justify the raised concern. The only thing that

---

[91] Anthony S. Fauci et al., "Covid-19—Navigating the Uncharted."

[92] "Coronavirus Is 10 Times More Lethal Than Seasonal Flu, Fauci Says," YouTube, March 11, 2020, https://www.youtube.com/watch?v=2DekzGCJhJw.

changed was the level of media obsession and panic being stoked at that time. Recall we were seeing things many of us had never seen before, at least not in this country, to the point we ran out of toilet paper. All of us were drinking from a fire hose in those days, so there frankly wasn't time to closely scrutinize Fauci's evolving claims. Nor was there anyone inside the White House really capable of doing so anyway. As for his reasoning, perhaps Fauci was simply reading the room. The media room, that is. As time went on, it seemed as if Fauci was at least as concerned with the media as he was the real-time data and science. That's a pattern that showed up frequently.

How much did you trust Fauci?

VERITAS: Early on we trusted him completely. He was a doctor and a scientist who had been around forever. If you spent any time in Washington at all, you learn to become pretty cynical. But you are supposed to be able to trust the doctors and scientists, right? Distrust started to mount over the mask issue when he admitted to lying. You can argue his reasoning was beneficial to the country, but he still admitted to lying. From that point on, the question every single person in the media should've been asking when Fauci made any declarative statement about the virus was how do we know he's not lying now? How do we know there's not some ulterior motive to what he's saying at this particular point? If he felt justified lying once, what's to stop him from feeling justified in lying again, and again?

Another thing you see in Washington is the media drug going to someone's head. I've always heard people in DC are starstruck by Hollywood stars and Hollywood stars are starstruck by DC elitists and officeholders. That attraction, to go from being a relatively obscure scientist in a world of pocket protectors, to Brad Pitt impersonating you on Saturday Night Live, is a drug many can't stop using once they've had their first hit. Fauci became a demigod of sorts to so many across the country. Not just because he's a reasonable sounding doctor, but because he would push back on the president they didn't like or feared. Except he was often pushing back on the very recommendations he gave that exact president in the first place. Eventually it became difficult to tell where coronavirus ended and the saga of Fauci began. Now he's on the cover of magazines. Now he's throwing out the first pitch at the Washington Nationals game. Now he's a pop culture tour de force. Fame is a drug few can stop, and when it became clear he was going to keep using that's when distrust built within the White House.

Were meetings at White House aggressive, passive aggressive? What was the dialogue like?

VERITAS: These meetings were often held in the situation room. They argued about language and data. It wasn't heated or overly angry, but there was clearly tension, especially as time went on and the real-time data didn't line up with the doomsday models. Fauci was a clear champion of shut it down and shut it down for a long time. Except as time went on, the real-time data didn't back that up. Unfortunately, by then it became obvious Fauci was quite enamored with his media persona. He would say things definitively there just wasn't any data yet for, or the data didn't confirm. He was never like, "Look folks, this is a novel virus and we're doing the best we can here." He spoke as a prophet or seer. Every opinion he had was definitive, even if it contradicted yesterday's opinion. I think this may be why he got so defensive when he got pushback from Senator Rand Paul, who's also a doctor. Because of Rand's credentials, he was about the only one who felt comfortable tugging on the hem of Fauci's garment. Clearly Fauci didn't like that very much. After all, the great and powerful Fauci is the go-to guy on every network.

And let's be real, the media loved every minute of it. It's not just media bias, but the media ratings matter, too. They have to blow this up, focus on the fight back and forth, and make the virus into the Malaysian flight that CNN kept on and on with. It has to be all catastrophic all of the time, or people will make their own decisions and go about their lives. And if there's anything the media in Washington cannot handle, it's the average American making decisions in their lives without its supposedly valuable input. So Fauci feeds off the media, and the media feeds off of Fauci. Both of them clinging to each other to make both of them more relevant.

What's the way out?

VERITAS: With Trump out of the White House, all of these various figures and entities have to rise and fall on their own merit now. They don't have Trump to collectively blame or hide behind. Take New York Governor Andrew Cuomo, for example. Fauci has a real weakness there, because they're seen as simpatico and Fauci has publicly praised him. Then there's the CDC, which has become a joke with its latest school recommendations when we can see real-time data from places where the schools were already opened and it just doesn't reconcile with CDC's claims. The more of this kind of information that comes out, the more people will ask what the hell was all this for? What were they doing? Look at these lies. Look at this information they kept from us or tried to push on us that just wasn't true, but they were so definitive about. People are going to be, well, pretty pissed off.

Chapter 6

Sweden: The Control Group That Never Was

One nation stood athwart the lockdown madness that infested the entire civilized world to some degree—Sweden.

How the nation that gave us Greta Thunberg's magical mystery tour of left-wing pseudo-religion—not-so-cleverly camouflaged as "climate science"—ended up being the greatest control group in the history of Western civilization is anyone's guess. Maybe it's as simple as the statists in Sweden, perhaps Europe's most secular and left-wing nation, already have all the power they want so they don't need to worry about letting a good crisis go to waste? They never needed to politicize this virus as a will to power, they already had it, so no point destroying your own country if you don't have to?

Regardless of motivation, hordes of American leftists who previously viewed Sweden as the model for the US to emulate have suddenly forgotten it actually exists. On the other hand, multitudes of conservatives and libertarians suddenly found themselves googling the prospect of relocating there. Politics makes for strange bedfellows, indeed.

But let's set the politics aside, and just look at the hard data, shall we? As far as the authors of this book are concerned, the truth is its own reward. So what does the truth say—did Sweden make the right call in defying the lockdown madness that swept the globe, by instead keeping its country mostly open despite the presence of coronavirus?

The authors of this book have combined for more than a quarter-century of experience covering and/or analyzing current events, and we have never seen a subject victimized by more gaslighting than Sweden and coronavirus. Sweden was like if hydroxychloroquine and Donald Trump had a baby. All the same people with an abnormally zealous desire for them both to fail projected their combined scorn upon poor Sweden. We personally witnessed numerous outright lies and distortions of Sweden's data with our own eyes during this pandemic.

And apparently at least some of it was coordinated. Two Swedish investigative media groups uncovered a closed Facebook group of two hundred–plus academics, thought leaders, researchers, and others who were conspiring about how to manifest their shared disdain for Sweden's defiance into critical messaging for distribution in global media.[93] This group reportedly had three main goals: (1) to influence the Swedish government's coronavirus policy; (2) to criticize positive media coverage of Sweden's coronavirus policy; (3) to damage Sweden's image around the world, as well as those who were formulating its coronavirus policy. Because nothing says you have the better argument quite like declaring an intifada.

Of course, they only hate 'cause they ain't you, as the kids say today. If Sweden's approach were a miserable failure, there would be no reason to organize the smearing of it. The results would speak for themselves and the country's leaders would be shamed in front of the world. However, agitprop is needed when you're peddling propaganda, not stone-cold facts that let the truth chips fall where they may. Sweden's cardinal sin was daring to provide the world a control group to either prove or disprove the effectiveness of lockdowns. And if there's anything we know unelected bureaucrats hate more than anything else, it's clearly defined provability. Clarity is the enemy of bureaucratic perpetuity.

As the world headed into the six-month mark of lockdowns, it was becoming impossible to ignore what was alternatively happening in Sweden:

---

[93] Johan Hellström (@jhnhellstrom), Twitter, February 9, 2021, https://twitter.com/jhnhellstrom/status/1359047086101176320.

> *The country's population-adjusted death rate, meanwhile, is in the top 10 worldwide, but lower than the rates for Italy, Spain and even New York, where heavy lockdowns prevailed.... According to the World Health Organization, Sweden's daily deaths peaked (three months ago) and have been declining ever since.*[94]

Let's take a look at Sweden's overall statistical profile.

From July 11, 2020, until October 26 (a period of 107 days) Sweden successfully failed to reach double-figures in daily deaths. While it is true the country's herd immunity hopes have yet to materialize, and like the rest of the world it was hit with a second seasonal wave that arrived during traditional flu-pneumonia season, at the time this book was being written Sweden's second wave was collapsing just as second waves were across the world where there were lockdowns. On December 28, 2020, Sweden reached a peak high with 121 daily deaths. But a month later that number had been cut in half by January 26, and then by February 21

---

[94] Daniel Payne, "After 6 Months without Lockdowns, Sweden's COVID-19 Deaths, Infections Bottom Out," Just the News, updated August 2, 2020, https://justthenews.com/politics-policy/coronavirus/after-6-months-no-lockdown-swedish-covid-deaths-bottomed-out.

Sweden was back down into the single digits with its daily deaths once again.[95]

And all this without punishing its people with lockdowns or masks. In fact, local governments in Sweden are even banning their people from wearing masks![96]

So how does Sweden compare with the rest of the world?[97]

As of February 23, 2021, Sweden was performing better than lockdown countries Italy, United Kingdom, Portugal, United States, Spain, Mexico, Peru, and France in deaths per one million population. In terms of total cases per one million population, Sweden was outperforming lockdown countries like the United States, Israel, Portugal, Spain, and Switzerland.

In other words, Sweden has outperformed the United States' policy being guided by Fauci within the two most important COVID-19 metrics—deaths and cases.

---

[95] "Sweden: Coronavirus Cases," Worldometer, March 4, 2021, https://www.worldometers.info/coronavirus/country/sweden/.
[96] Tine Walravens and Paul O'Shea, "COVID: Why Are Swedish Towns Banning Masks?" *The Conversation*, February 8, 2021, https://theconversation.com/covid-why-are-swedish-towns-banning-masks-153681.%20"COVID.
[97] "Sweden: Coronavirus Cases," Worldometers, March 4, 2021, https://www.worldometers.info/coronavirus/country/sweden/.

Sweden and Michigan have roughly the same population. As of February 23, 2021, the State of Michigan was reporting 639,712 total cases. Sweden was reporting 642,099 total cases. The State of Michigan was reporting 16,380 deaths with COVID-19. Sweden was reporting 12,719. And yet, unlike Sweden which remained mostly open, Michigan imposed one of the harshest lockdowns in the US. Even to the point of banning the sales of seeds and home gardening supplies in an all-out effort to keep its citizens quarantined indoors. [98] Michigan is still overcoming the fallout of its unusually harsh lockdown. Almost one-third of its businesses have been shuttered,[99] and the state suffered the worst job losses in the country.[100]

So while Sweden sustained a 0.4 percent increase in total cases by comparison, Michigan suffered a 28 percent increase of deaths compared to Sweden—on top of its ongoing economic turmoil. On the other hand, Sweden's mild 2.9

---

[98] Nick Sibilla, "Michigan Bans Many Stores from Selling Seeds, Home Gardening Supplies, Calls Them 'Not Necessary,'" *Forbes*, April 16, 2020, https://www.forbes.com/sites/nicksibilla/2020/04/16/michigan-bans-many-stores-from-selling-seeds-home-gardening-supplies-calls-them-not-necessary/?sh=4141bf875f80.

[99] Kyle Olson, "Gretchen Whitmer Lockdown Closed 32% of Michigan Businesses," Breitbart, December 18, 2020, https://www.breitbart.com/politics/2020/12/18/gretchen-whitmer-lockdown-closed-32-of-michigan-businesses/.

[100] Kyle Olson, "Michigan Suffers Worst Job Losses in U.S. amid Gretchen Whitmer Lockdown," Breitbart, January 28, 2021, https://www.breitbart.com/politics/2021/01/28/michigan-suffers-worst-job-losses-us-gretchen-whitmer-lockdown/.

percent contraction to its GDP in 2020 was 151 percent *less* than the average economic decline seen throughout the entirety of European Union countries that use the Euro as their main currency.[101]

Sweden, the control group, seems to at the very least indicate "the virus is gonna virus" as former *New York Times* reporter Alex Berenson is fond of saying. In other words, regardless of mass lockdowns or not, Sweden at least seems to indicate the virus is going to do its thing until we reach herd immunity—either through natural immunity or vaccination. Therefore, it's really pointless to destroy your own economy and eradicate civil liberties with so little promise of a return on investment.

"We can live with the truth [virus is gonna virus] or destroy ourselves with the lie of perfect control," Berenson said.[102]

That doesn't mean isolating vulnerable demographics should be abandoned, and you just let the virus run roughshod through your country, as lockdown apologists claim. Not even Sweden went without any mitigations. But these sorts of false

---

[101] "Swedish Govt Sees Milder Downturn in 2020, Slower Growth Next Year," Reuters, December 16, 2020, https://www.reuters.com/article/sweden-economy/swedish-govt-sees-milder-downturn-in-2020-slower-growth-next-year-idUSKBN28Q1VZ?il=0.

[102] Alex Berenson (@AlexBerenson), Twitter, November 1, 2020, https://twitter.com/alexberenson/status/1322920135808569344?lang=en.

choices represent childlike thinking. Adults understand complex problems often require nuanced solutions. The ability to walk and chew gum at the same time.

Which means there must be a way for the world's largest economy, the United States, to both protect those who face a clear and present danger from coronavirus and maintain a way of life the whole world depends upon, not just its own citizens. That the country which gave the world the light bulb, indoor plumbing, radio, television, microchips, semiconductors, antibiotics, manned flight, and a man on the moon could probably figure how to fight a virus with a 1.7 percent case fatality rate without causing a near-depression and constitutional crisis.

By August 1, 2020, we already knew the following about COVID-19:

85 and older are just 3.2% of the U.S. population but they make up 33% of all Covid deaths…75 and older are just 7% of the U.S. population but they make up 59% of all Covid deaths…54 and younger are 70% of the U.S population but they make up just 8% of all Covid deaths…Covid deaths don't even register until we reach ages 15-24 and then it is only 0.2% of all Covid deaths. So kids kindergarten through college undergrad face no significant threat of death due to Covid.[103]

Again, we knew this information by August 1, 2020. So how is it possible that heading into March of 2021, a full seven months later, we're still fighting to have our kids in school and businesses open in way too much of this country? Or to not have to wear a useless Chinese face diaper (more on that in a later chapter) if we want to go almost anywhere?

Those in power, like Fauci, have known for quite some time now this virus targets the elderly and those with select preexisting conditions. So why didn't we put a singular focus on protecting those people? Our failure to do so, and concentrate so much government power on endlessly locking down the healthy instead, still didn't stop 45 percent of all COVID-19 deaths coming from America's nursing homes and long-term care facilities.[104] That is frankly indefensible. We supposedly locked down the healthy to stop them from asymptomatically infecting grandma, and grandma was often killed anyway.

---

[103] "150 Days Later: COVID Facts the Media Isn't Telling You," *Steve Deace Show*, YouTube, August 13, 2020, https://www.youtube.com/watch?v=uT3HniJ8J6A.
[104] Avik Roy, "Nursing Home Deaths from COVID-19: U.S. Historical Data," FREOPP, July 15, 2020, https://freopp.org/nursing-home-deaths-from-covid-19-u-s-historical-data-b4ad44cfc48e.

While Fauci is the focus of this book, as we stated in the introduction he is but a construct of a problematic system. Had he not been here, the system would've just put forth someone else. Maybe someone better at this, or worse, but still unelected and largely unaccountable. See, too many of the representatives we elect love judicial supremacy, bureaucratic supremacy, or nongovernment-agency supremacy. For if such entities are the ones calling the shots, our politicians can escape voter scrutiny for the fallout for their decisions. Holding the political class accountable becomes akin to trying to nail Jell-O to a door. And that's just what most incumbent politicians prefer, because they also seek self-perpetuation above all.

Sweden's effort is also largely run by one unelected bureaucrat named Anders Tegnell. It just so happened that he has pursued real science and actual data, while balancing the broader concerns about preserving his country's way of life. But what would Sweden's way of life be like if he had not? What if he pursued, instead, whatever in the literal Hell that Fauci has been after? Then it's quite likely we wouldn't have ever had Sweden as a control group, and our ability to end these useless and immoral lockdowns would be further diminished minus a real-world example to the contrary.

That's why the answer here isn't as simple as replacing a Fauci with a Tegnell, any more than you fight a revolution to replace a King George III with a King George Washington.

The constitutional republic we were founded to be views such concentrated power in the hands of one person, whether vain or empathetic, as anathema to liberty.

Unfortunately, that anathema has become our new normal.

Chapter 7

The Wuhan Lab

There's a lot we still do not know for certain about the true origins of the novel coronavirus, but there is one thing we do know for sure. The National Institute of Allergy and Infectious Diseases, which is led by Anthony Fauci, funded the Wuhan Institute of Virology in China for "gain of function research on bat coronaviruses."[105]

According to the US Department of Health and Human Services, gain of function research is used to "help define the fundamental nature of human-pathogen interactions, thereby enabling assessment of the pandemic potential of emerging infectious agents, informing public health and preparedness efforts, and furthering medical countermeasure development. Gain-of-function studies may entail biosafety and biosecurity

---

[105] Fred Guteri, "Dr. Fauci Backed Controversial Wuhan Lab with U.S. Dollars for Risky Coronavirus Research," *Newsweek*, April 28, 2020, https://www.newsweek.com/dr-fauci-backed-controversial-wuhan-lab-millions-us-dollars-risky-coronavirus-research-1500741.

risks; therefore, the risks and benefits of gain-of-function research must be evaluated."[106]

That last sentence is especially of interest, since there have been scores of rumors (often dismissed by the scientific community [107]) the novel coronavirus virus may have accidentally escaped from a research lab, if not outright engineered in one. Tucker Carlson of Fox News noted the intermediate horseshoe bat, originally thought to have transmitted it, "was not available at the Wuhan wet market" and its "native populations were no closer than 600 miles away from the first known cases making a natural transmission from bat to human appear more unlikely."[108] Trump White House sources also fueled speculation about a Wuhan laboratory origin for the novel coronavirus as well.[109]

---

[106] "Gain-of-Function Research," Public Health Emergency, US Department of Health & Human Services,
https://www.phe.gov/s3/dualuse/Pages/GainOfFunction.aspx.
[107] Michael Marshall, "Did Coronavirus Come from a Lab?" *New Scientist*,
https://www.newscientist.com/term/coronavirus-come-lab/.
[108] Virginia Kruta, "Tucker Carlson Airs Report Claiming Coronavirus 'Probably Originated from a Laboratory in Wuhan,'" *Daily Caller*, March 31, 2020, https://dailycaller.com/2020/03/31/coronavirus-lab-wuhan-tucker-carlson-report/.
[109] Bret Baier and Gregg Re, "Sources Believe Coronavirus Outbreak Originated in Wuhan Lab as Part of China's Efforts to Compete with US," Fox News, April 15, 2020, https://www.foxnews.com/politics/coronavirus-wuhan-lab-china-compete-us-sources.

Which brings us back to Fauci's funding of the Wuhan Institute of Virology. *Newsweek*, which was the first to break this story, provided the following details:

> *In 2019, with the backing of the NIAID (run by Fauci), the National Institutes of Health committed $3.7 million over six years for research that included some gain-of-function work. The program followed another $3.7 million, 5-year project for collecting and studying bat coronaviruses, which ended in 2019, bringing the total to $7.4 million. Many scientists have criticized gain of function research, which involves manipulating viruses in the lab to explore their potential for infecting humans, because it creates a risk of starting a pandemic from accidental release…(Research) included additional surveillance work but also gain-of-function research for the purpose of understanding how bat coronaviruses could mutate to attack humans… The project proposal states: "We will use S protein sequence data, infectious clone technology, in vitro and in vivo infection experiments and analysis of receptor binding to test the hypothesis that % divergence thresholds in S protein sequences predict spillover potential." In layman's terms, "spillover potential" **refers to the ability of a virus to jump from animals to humans**, which requires that the virus be able to attach to receptors in the cells of humans. SARS-CoV-2, for instance, is adept at binding to the*

ACE2 receptor in human lungs and other organs.[110]
[emphasis added]

The *Newsweek* story goes on to cite scientists at Rutgers and Johns Hopkins who were critical of this kind of research and also pointed out the Obama administration pressured Fauci's organization to cancel this research effort back in 2014. The moratorium was lifted by the NIH in 2017, and shortly after this *Newsweek* report the Trump administration demanded the rest of the research be cancelled, too.[111]

About nine months after the initial furor over this story died down, Steve Hilton at Fox News resurrected it with his own investigation. Hilton found six payments to the Wuhan Institute of Virology from the NIH to fund gain-of-function research despite the funding ban, as well as the NIH denying they were involved. "It's a different project with a different (project) number," Hilton pointed out about the NIH's denial. "They're right to say this project does not include gain of function research, but that's not the one we asked about. The one we asked about does contain gain of function research.

---

[110] Fred Guteri, "Dr. Fauci Backed Controversial Wuhan Lab."
[111] David Lim and Brianna Ehley, "Fauci Says White House Told NIH to Cancel Funding for Bat Virus Study," *Politico*, June 23, 2020, https://www.politico.com/news/2020/06/23/fauci-nih-white-house-bat-study-336452.

The statement we received from the NIH is totally deceptive."[112]

Hilton's investigation also found "the Wuhan Institute of Virology then began to genetically engineer viruses from the feces of bats and infected human cells with the virus." Hilton explained, "The genetic changes they made in the lab, unlocked a highly specific doorway into the human body. The virus that causes Covid-19 uses that exact same doorway." Hilton went on to point out the "Chinese regime replaced the head of the Wuhan Institute of Virology with the Chinese head of the bioweapons program and vital evidence was promptly destroyed."[113]

Finally, Hilton connected the dots of what you have to believe to accept the novel coronavirus is just a random act of bad luck mutation/transmission:

> *To swallow the natural transmission theory, you have to believe the bat or other animal or infected human would have to travel 1,000 miles from its habitat without infecting anybody until it reached Wuhan,*

[112] Annaliese Levy, "Steve Hilton Reveals New Evidence Linking COVID-19 Origins to US-Funded Research in China," *The Sara Carter Show*, February 1, 2021, https://saraacarter.com/steve-hilton-reveals-new-evidence-linking-covid-19-origins-to-us-funded-research-in-china/.

[113] Annaliese Levy, "Steve Hilton Reveals Explosive Evidence on COVID-19 Origins and the Fauci Connection," *The Sara Carter Show*, January 25, 2021, https://saraacarter.com/steve-hilton-reveals-explosive-evidence-on-covid-19-origins-and-the-fauci-connection/.

> *where it was already 10-20 times more infectious than any previous virus occurring in nature, and it just happened to arrive at the only lab in China working on that very virus.*[114]

Perhaps now is a good time to remind you that back on January 14, 2020, the World Health Organization tweeted out to the world its reassurance "preliminary investigations conducted by the Chinese authorities have found no clear evidence of human-to-human transmission of the novel coronavirus."[115]

Amazingly, that tweet was still up on the WHO's official Twitter account at the time this book was being written.

Almost a year later, on February 10, 2021, the WHO then concluded the novel coronavirus "most likely originated in animals before spreading to humans, and dismissed a theory that the disease had been leaked by a laboratory in the Chinese city of Wuhan."[116] What was the WHO's basis for this conclusion?

---

[114] Annaliese Levy, "Steve Hilton Reveals Explosive Evidence on COVID-19 Origins."

[115] World Health Organization (@WHO), "Preliminary investigations conducted by the Chinese authorities have found no clear evidence of human-to-human transmission of the novel #coronavirus (2019-nCoV) Identified in #Wuhan, #China." January 14, 2020, https://twitter.com/WHO/status/1217043229427761152.

[116] Sam Meredith, "WHO Says Covid 'Most Likely' Originated in Animals and Spread to Humans, Dismisses Lab Leak Theory," CNBC, February 9, 2021,

"The Chinese Communist Party told them it didn't," US Senator Ted Cruz said bluntly, while calling the WHO "shameful" and a "propagandist" for China.[117]

Just days before the WHO attempted to absolve China of any responsibility for the pandemic it exported to the rest of the world, the *New York Times* swooned that China "was the only major economy that has returned to steady growth." Even going so far as to regurgitate CCP talking points like "China's successes in each dimension of the pandemic—medical, diplomatic and economic—have reinforced its conviction **that an __authoritarian__ capacity** [emphasis added] to quickly mobilize people and resources gave the country a decisive edge."[118]

Again that quote is from perhaps the most influential newspaper in the United States, and not a propaganda leaflet dropped in the streets of Beijing—but you'd be hard-pressed to tell the difference.

Which bring us full circle back to the funding of the Wuhan Institute of Virology.

---

https://www.cnbc.com/2021/02/09/who-outlines-wuhan-findings-on-origins-of-covid-pandemic.html.
[117] Ted Cruz (@tedcruz), February 10, 2021,
https://twitter.com/tedcruz/status/1359505175816372225.
[118] New York Times (@nytimes), February 5, 2021,
https://twitter.com/nytimes/status/1357603818150662147.

On February 21, 2021, the *New York Post* editorial board was incredulous to learn "the Wuhan Institute of Virology remains the most likely source of the coronavirus pandemic, yet it is set to receive U.S. taxpayer dollars for the next three years. Worse, the cash will fund more animal research."[119] *The Daily Caller* also discovered the president of an organization who was assisting in the controversial gain of function research at the Wuhan Institute of Virology "was the sole U.S. member in the World Health Organization delegation that investigated the origins of Covid-19 in China."[120]

Clearly no conflict of interest there.

Going back to the introduction of this book, and at other places throughout, we have stressed that while Fauci is the focal point of this effort he is also merely a construct and byproduct of a swampy bureaucracy that is largely unaccountable and unelected. The story of the ongoing funding of the Wuhan Institute of Virology testifies to this inconvenient truth. This is a story that Fauci plays a part in, yes, but also goes far beyond him. Fauci is a servant of this leviathan; he is not the leviathan himself. He is neither our

---

[119] *Post* Editorial Board, "Wuhan Lab at Heart of COVID Outbreak May Get Three More Years of US Funding," *New York Post*, February 21, 2021, https://nypost.com/2021/02/21/wuhan-lab-at-heart-of-covid-outbreak-may-get-more-us-funding/.
[120] *New York Post*, "Wuhan Lab at Heart of COVID Outbreak."

cure for the coronavirus nor the cause of the bureaucratic disease.

Nevertheless it is instructive to take an in-depth look at Fauci, his motivations, and his associations (such as the Wuhan Institute of Virology) as a means of learning just how far down the rabbit hole goes. When it comes to the Wuhan Institute of Virology, at the very least he should be asked to give an account of the potential dangers of gain-of-function research, how extensive his knowledge is of what went on there, and the true origin of the virus. Instead, he's hardly been questioned about these things at all, but he has given plenty of opinions about when it's safe to play professional sports or when to double-mask.

For example, how many of you reading this book had ever even heard of gain-of-function research before coming to this chapter? And yet it could very well end up becoming the explanation for the origin of the pandemic that has threatened our way of life more than 9/11. This should've been among the first lines of questioning for Fauci to answer in front of the country, especially because the initial story that broke the news of this funding goes all the way back to the first two months of the lockdowns.

Here's another example you probably also didn't know. On March 1, 2021, Judicial Watch and *The Daily Caller* received "301 pages of emails and other records of Dr.

Anthony Fauci and Dr. H. Clifford Lane from U.S. Department of Health and Human Services showing that National Institutes of Health (NIH) officials tailored confidentiality forms to China's terms and that the World Health Organization (WHO) conducted an unreleased, 'strictly confidential' COVID-19 epidemiological analysis in January 2020."[121]

These emails were obtained via a Freedom of Information lawsuit filed in U.S. District Court by Judicial Watch, after the U.S. Department of Health and Human Services refused to voluntarily respond to requests for the documents going back to April 1, 2020. Now why would they do that?

The emails include a conversation about confidentiality forms on February 14–15, 2020, that were "tailored to China's terms so we cannot use the ones from before."[122] Can't we all agree that tailoring things to China's concerns always ends well?

Another email dated March 4, 2020, points out inconsistencies between the World Health Organization-China joint mission report and the Wuhan Public Health Committee.

---

[121] "Judicial Watch: New Emails Detail WHO/NIH Accommodations to Chinese Confidentiality 'Terms,'" Judicial Watch, March 1, 2021, https://www.judicialwatch.org/press-releases/emails-who-terms/?utm_source=twitter&utm_medium=social&utm_campaign=press_releas e.
[122] "DCNF v HHS Nov 2020 00149 pg 161," Judicial Watch, February 26, 2021, https://www.judicialwatch.org/documents/dcnf-v-hhs-nov-2020-00149-pg-161/.

The latter of which admits "from Jan. 11th to 17th there were new clinically diagnosed and confirmed cases every day in Wuhan, which is not consistent with Wuhan Public Health Committee's numbers."[123]

Ethan Barton, editor-in-chief of *The Daily Caller*, said "these emails set the tone early on in the coronavirus outbreak. It's clear that the WHO allowed China to control the information flow from the start. True transparency is crucial."

And yet, Fauci voiced his support for the WHO after President Trump terminated our relationship with the organization because he didn't trust it.[124]

According to Judicial Watch President Tom Fitton, whose organization is spearheading the continuing investigation into communications between our healthcare policy bureaucracy led by Fauci and others around the globe, "These new emails show WHO and Fauci's NIH special accommodations to Chinese communist efforts to control information about COVID-19."

---

[123] "DCNF v HHS Nov 2020 00149 pgs 194-196," Judicial Watch, February 26, 2021, https://www.judicialwatch.org/documents/dcnf-v-hhs-nov-2020-00149-pgs-195-196/.

[124] Paul LeBlanc, "Fauci Voices Support for World Health Organization after Trump Terminates US Relationship," CNN, June 11, 2020, https://www.cnn.com/2020/06/11/politics/fauci-world-health-organization-coronavirus/index.html.

If that has *any* chance of being true, that Fauci's organization provided "special accommodations" to the country that infected the world with this novel coronavirus, don't we deserve to know? Shouldn't that be investigated thoroughly?

If there's anything being governed by an all-powerful bureaucracy has taught us, it is this: too much money, too much power, and too little accountability/transparency among the unelected are not a recipe for sustaining a constitutional republic.

Chapter 8

Andrew Cuomo, the First Bishop of Faucism

False messiahs inspire apostles, too. Among those apostles there must also be a leader.

To the Branch Covidian cult, more on that later, Anthony Fauci is alpha and omega. However, in his corporeal form not even the great and powerful Fauci is omnipresent. Therefore, he needs proxies. Those who will be his vicars, and rule in his stead while he's busy doing whatever the Hell it is he does most days—other than endless fawning media appearances. Enter New York Governor Andrew Cuomo, whose political future was imperiled at the time this book was being written for heinous reasons we're about to discuss.

Upon this type of sludge Fauci has built his church, and if he has any say not even the data or decency will prevail against it. Yet Cuomo is a major problem for Fauci. For he's arguably more than a disciple, but a progeny. He has emulated Fauci's penchant for turning shamelessness and gaslighting into a cottage industry for self-promotion. Except Cuomo is also an unlikable and prickly politician, who lacks the charm and capability to absorb endless compliments with an "aw shucks" false humility as Fauci so deftly does.

Which is also why when Cuomo has the chutzpah to write a book[125] about his "leadership lessons learned" from the pandemic and then go on a book tour during a pandemic as schools and businesses remained closed in his state, it raises his own threat level.[126] As a politician who needs the votes of the people, Cuomo cannot afford to stay in his lane. He must, instead, invade yours. He cannot afford to just raise his profile, but must expand it. The few times Fauci's standing has been imperiled is when he's attempted the same, like his ridiculously embarrassing first pitch at the Washington Nationals game,[127] followed by being captured with his mask off as he watched the rest of the game from the stands.[128]

Fauci's public persona took a massive hit after that, which provided the opportunity for the Trump administration to

[125] Andrew Cuomo, *American Crisis: Leadership Lessons from the COVID-19 Pandemic* (New York: Crown, 2020).
[126] Tara Francis Chan and Elizabeth Weill-Greenberg, "New York Governor Andrew Cuomo Is Fresh off His Book Tour, but Activists Say He Doesn't Live Up to His National Reputation," The Appeal, November 19, 2020, https://theappeal.org/andrew-cuomo-covid-19-pandemic-criticism/.
[127] "Dr. Anthony Fauci Tosses Out First Pitch," YouTube, July 23, 2020, https://www.youtube.com/watch?v=0Rr9XC3hNGg.
[128] Travis Pittman, "Fauci Calls Criticism over Photo of Him with Mask Down 'Mischievous,'" WUSA9, July 24, 2020, https://www.wusa9.com/article/news/health/coronavirus/anthony-fauci-face-mask-down-photo-coronavirus/507-e33379cb-d79e-479b-9960-13293c96572f.

finally (and we would argue long overdue) marginalize his presence—if only temporarily. Afterwards, Fauci seemed to learn his lesson. As long as he plays to the brand of "the nation's leading infectious disease expert" he has no rival and can largely go unchallenged. Not because he possesses the superior expertise, mind you, but the superior platform over those that do. Step outside that prism, however, and all bets are off.

On the other hand, Cuomo would not be the first politician to prove that self-awareness is dead. Thus, when you brag on yourself about how great your pandemic leadership was, and expand your public persona from king to doctor-savior-king, a little thing like the fact you may have helped murder thousands of nursing home residents in your own state is going to prove once more that blowback can be a female dog.[129]

So what does this have to do with Fauci? Quite a bit, actually.

See, it was Fauci who previously bestowed honor about Cuomo's claims of self-canonization. On July 20, 2020, Fauci appeared on PBS and all but said of Cuomo "this is my son in whom I am well pleased" when he said the following:

---

[129] Gabrielle Fonrouge, "'It Looked Like Murder': Families of Nursing Home Victims Demand Cuomo Probe," *New York Post*, February 15, 2021, https://nypost.com/2021/02/15/families-of-nursing-home-victims-demand-probe-of-cuomo/.

> *We know that, when you do it properly, you bring down*
> *those cases. We have done it. We have done it in New*
> *York. New York got hit worse than any place in the*
> *world. And they did it correctly by doing the things [I*
> *recommended].*[130]

Almost exactly one month to the day after Fauci credited Cuomo with such righteousness, New York's ambitious governor took that blessing and announced his forthcoming book, *American Crisis*, meant to make him the political face of COVID heroics. Translation: Cuomo would be the poster-child for Faucism.[131]

The book, of course, became a bestseller. And with Joe Biden safely inaugurated into the White House, Fauci then found the earliest opportunity he could to troll his old boss Trump.

"The idea that you can get up here and…let the science speak, it is somewhat of a liberating feeling," Fauci smugly

---

[130] "Coronavirus News: Dr. Fauci Says New York 'Did It Correctly,'" ABC7 NY, July 20, 2020, https://abc7ny.com/covid-19-ny-fauci-anthony-cuomo/6324584/.

[131] Hillel Italie, "Gov. Andrew Cuomo Book on COVID-19 Response Out in October," Associated Press News, August 18, 2020, https://apnews.com/article/election-2020-virus-outbreak-democratic-national-convention-new-york-andrew-cuomo-e04b9f8f9d87277f93cdbbfc1428694f.

said during one of his first appearances on behalf of the new administration.[132]

Oh really?

Did Cuomo allegedly leading thousands of vulnerable elderly to their deaths inside COVID-infected nursing homes "let the science speak"? We doubt their loved ones were left with a "liberating feeling."

Because "liberated" isn't how Fauci seemed when asked to comment as Cuomo's increasingly obvious culpability in those deaths mounted, not to mention his repeatedly lying about it.[133] But as another fellow famous New Yorker, George Costanza, once infamously said, "It's not a lie if you believe it." Should we expect Cuomo to display any level of remorse or humility whatsoever, when he had already been baptized and knighted in public by America's most powerful bureaucrat?

Cuomo aide Melissa DeRosa finally flat-out admitted to state lawmakers—almost a year after Cuomo's mistakes

---

[132] Maureen Groppe, "Fauci Unleashed: He Says It's 'Liberating' That He Can 'Let the Science Speak' as Adviser to Biden," *USA Today*, MSN News, January 22, 2021, https://www.msn.com/en-us/news/politics/dr-fauci-says-letting-the-science-speak-is-liberating-after-serving-under-trump/ar-BB1cYCgT.

[133] Bernadette Hogan, Carl Campanile, and Bruce Golding, "Cuomo Aide Melissa DeRosa Admits They Hid Nursing Home Data So Feds Wouldn't Find Out," *New York Post*, February 11, 2021, https://nypost.com/2021/02/11/cuomo-aide-admits-they-hid-nursing-home-data-from-feds/.

needlessly began to fill body bags—that data on the number of deaths in such facilities was purposefully underreported **by more than six thousand people** in order to minimize potential fallout in the press. In other words, Cuomo deceived to protect his public persona during the pandemic. How is that any different than what we've exhaustively footnoted and detailed Fauci has been doing all along? Maybe Fauci's duplicity didn't directly lead to the deaths of people as it allegedly did with Cuomo, but Fauci's con has casualties, too. How many family businesses will never reopen? How many benchmarks of life were postponed and never made up? How many suicides and increased depressions? How far behind are our kids in school?

So go ahead, Dr. Fauci. By all means, liberate the science for all of us plebes. Or at least for those of your fellow New Yorkers who will never sadly see their loved ones again.

"I can't," Fauci said when finally asked about the scandal that threatened to topple Cuomo. "I mean, I'm sorry. I'm really—I'm honestly not trying to evade your question, but I'm not really sure of all the details of that, and I think if I make a statement, it probably could either be incorrect or taken out of context. So, I prefer not to comment on that."[134]

---

[134] Trent Baker, "Fauci: 'I Prefer Not to Comment' on Gov. Cuomo Mishandling Coronavirus," Breitbart, February 16, 2021, https://www.breitbart.com/clips/2021/02/16/fauci-i-prefer-not-to-comment-on-gov-cuomo-mishandling-coronavirus/.

Weird. To paraphrase the great philosopher Inigo Montoya, we don't think "liberate" means what Fauci thinks it means. He seems to be confusing it with "deception" or "cowardice."

We also don't think a man who is up to his eyeballs in funding research in Wuhan, China, of all places[135]—the very birthplace of COVID-19—can get away with saying he doesn't have a clue what is going on in his own home state, as it was ravaged as hard by the Wuhan virus as any other place on earth. He can't have it both ways. Fauci cannot provide legitimacy to Cuomo's prior grandiose claims, thus playing de facto kingmaker, and then feign ignorance or sheepishly demur when the macabre reality of what actually occurred is brought to light. On second thought, he could, but that would be cosmically dishonest.

Furthermore, among Cuomo's defenses for his state's nursing home disaster in 2020 was that he was merely following federal guidelines. Now how would a guy like Cuomo, who seems aggressively prone to doing whatever he wants whenever he wants to, suddenly feel it would be a compelling narrative to play the victim card?

---

[135] Joe Tacopino, "Dr. Fauci Backed Funding for Controversial Wuhan Lab Studying Origin of Coronavirus," *New York Post*, April 29, 2020, https://nypost.com/2020/04/29/dr-fauci-backed-controversial-wuhan-lab-studying-coronavirus/.

Perhaps because by gaining the aforementioned blessing of Fauci, Cuomo *was* receiving absolution from the federal government. Fauci *was*, for all intents and purposes, the federal government when it came to COVID for far too long in the final year of the Trump administration. Trump abrogated too much of his authority to Fauci, as we've already discussed, and didn't reclaim his power and rally the country back to normalcy until it was too late to save his presidency.

And with Biden now in the White House, Fauci is ascendant again.

It was such a successful endorsement by Fauci in the eyes of those who have birthed a cult around him, that later on when December arrived Cuomo and Fauci were invited by the press to ham it up together and appoint themselves the "modern-day De Niro and Pacino" of virus fighters.[136]

Let's set aside the irony that those two great actors have accumulated two of the highest body counts in their films in cinematic history; it's almost like Fauci and Cuomo have been perfecting their little rascals routine for some time now. Like they've been friends forever. Maybe because, you know, they've been friends forever.

---

[136] Bernadette Hogan and Kate Sheehy, "Cuomo Calls Fauci, Himself the Pacino and De Niro of COVID-19 Era," *New York Post*, December 7, 2020, https://nypost.com/2020/12/07/cuomo-compares-fauci-himself-to-pacino-and-de-niro-amid-covid/.

Back in May 2020, Governor Cuomo's brother, CNN host Chris Cuomo, was paid daily phone calls by Fauci after he contracted COVID-19—and then proceeded to hack the light fantastic from his televised basement during his quarantine. The calls were the kind of thing you do, Fauci said, when you've known the Cuomos since Chris "was almost a kid."[137]

"I care about you and was worried about you," Fauci told Chris Cuomo at the time. "I don't think that people were really experiencing or realizing how you were really sucking it up to look relatively normal. But when you finished the show, and we would start chatting at 11, 11:30 at night, you were wiped out and I was concerned."

Indeed, these are always the conversations had among those who are just casual, barely-know-you relations, or not. So, no, Fauci cannot now claim detachment from whatever kind of ghoul Andrew Cuomo may turn out to be. Dr. Frankenstein cannot reject the monster he created.

It comes down to this: if Cuomo is guilty then it was Fauci driving the getaway car. The minute that book was announced, or even published, Fauci could've diagnosed the governor's tall tale as a tell-tale heart, but he didn't. Nor can

---

[137] Tamar Lapin, "Why Chris Cuomo Got Daily Calls from Anthony Fauci While Fighting Coronavirus," *New York Post*, May 5, 2020, https://nypost.com/2020/05/05/dr-fauci-called-chris-cuomo-daily-during-coronavirus-ordeal/.

he claim lack of knowledge. On May 23, 2020, almost two full months before Fauci went on PBS to anoint Cuomo's New York as a paragon of rightness, the Associated Press released its initial report claiming thousands of unreported deaths inside New York's nursing homes as a result of Cuomo's policy.[138]

And yet, two months later, Fauci gave New York (and by extension its governor) a very public attaboy anyway. Given the amount of media attention the AP report generated, and the fact the AP is the mouth of the mainstream media river, it would be close to impossible to believe Fauci was not aware of it when he was later exalting Cuomo and New York.

Nor did Fauci take umbrage with Cuomo winning an actual Emmy for his daily propaganda briefings, which he held all the while knowing there were thousands of body bags we had yet to learn about. After all, game recognize game. However, Fauci did throw a hissy fit when then-President Trump ran a campaign ad featuring Fauci's own words—"I can't imagine that anybody could be doing more"[139]—about the performance of the Trump administration's White House coronavirus task force.

---

[138] Bernard Condon, Jennifer Peltz, and Jim Mustian, "AP Count: Over 4,300 Virus Patients Sent to NY Nursing Homes," CBS6 Albany, May 22, 2020, https://cbs6albany.com/news/local/ap-count-over-4300-virus-patients-sent-to-ny-nursing-homes.

[139] Andrew O'Reilly, "Fauci Says His Comments in New Trump Ad 'Were Taken Out of Context' and without His Permission," Fox News, October 11, 2020, https://www.foxnews.com/politics/fauci-comments-out-of-context.

"In my nearly five decades of public service, I have never publicly endorsed any political candidate," Fauci incredulously complained, as if he were suddenly aghast at the notion of being politically pimped out. "The comments attributed to me without my permission in the GOP campaign ad were taken out of context."

Let's check the Fauci scoreboard, then, shall we?

Letting Cuomo wash the blood from his hands 1, admitting Trump wasn't actually Hitler 0. The bottom line is that Fauci isn't so much an "expert" at picking fights with the virus he is charged with defeating, as he is with self-promotion and gaslighting—which may be why he and Cuomo get along so well.

The apple doesn't fall very far from the tree.

Chapter 9

Maskerade

Let it never be forgotten that on March 8, 2020, as fear of the pandemic was beginning to escalate and one week before "15 days to flatten the curve" was launched, Anthony Fauci told the country on *60 Minutes* "people should not be walking around with masks. There's no reason to be walking around with a mask."[140] And later Fauci admitted to *InStyle* magazine he lied when he said this, and didn't regret it, because "we have a serious problem with the lack of masks for the health providers."[141]

Before we venture into the combustible and divisive discussion of masks it is vitally important to set the stage for how the conversation first began—with Fauci's dishonesty. Either he lied as he admitted to the American people from the

---

[140] "March 2020: Dr. Anthony Fauci Talks with Dr. Jon LaPook about Covid-19," YouTube, March 8, 2020,
https://www.youtube.com/watch?v=PRa6t_e7dgI.
[141] Grace Panetta, "Fauci Says He Doesn't Regret Telling Americans Not to Wear Masks at the Beginning of the Pandemic," Business Insider, July 16, 2020, https://www.businessinsider.com/fauci-doesnt-regret-advising-against-masks-early-in-pandemic-2020-7.

outset for reasons he attempted to justify later, or his justification itself was the lie so he could reconcile his newfound mask zealotry with the position he previously took.

Perhaps no aspect of the COVID-19 conversation is more fraught with confusion than is the maskerade. There have been so many audacious and ridiculous claims about their effectiveness, it's become almost impossible to separate fact from fiction. But this is what happens when something as simple as a cloth mask becomes a talisman, or totem, for a cause. Such words are usually connected to religious imagery, and make no mistake a segment of the country has become religiously devoted to the mask.

And you can hardly blame them, when you have former CDC Director Robert Redfield—whom Fauci vouched for as a "talented and committed physician/scientist" who is "highly-regarded" when he was appointed by President Trump[142]— making such stupendously ridiculous claims as this before the US Congress:

> *I am going to comment as the CDC director that face masks, these face masks, are the most important public health tool we have. And I will continue to appeal to all*

---

[142] Ed Yong, "Trump's Pick for CDC Director Is Experienced but Controversial," *The Atlantic*, March 22, 2020, https://www.theatlantic.com/science/archive/2018/03/trumps-pick-for-cdc-director-is-experienced-but-controversial/556202/.

Americans, all individuals in our country, to embrace these face coverings. I might even go so far as to say that **this face mask is more guaranteed to protect me against Covid than when I take the Covid vaccine.**[143] *[emphasis added]*

Folks, either the COVID vaccines must suck or that is not science, that is a religious appeal. And one based on emotion and lacking reason at that. If that is true, then how come we haven't been wearing masks every flu season our entire lives?

For what Redfield and Fauci now claim about masks to be true, means your doctor has clearly been trying to kill you all along. Or is suicidal. Or both. Other than that, situation normal. Everything's fine. We're all fine here. How are you?

We simply don't remember a flu season when we saw doctors regularly wearing masks as a routine preventive measure, dear reader, do you? Not at casual doctor's office visits (where the flu is more dangerous to children than COVID). Not at parent-teacher conferences or youth sports games (my God, why do doctors hate children so much?). Not at the golf course (foursome or death wish, you decide).

---

[143] Caitlin O'Kane, "CDC Director Says Face Masks May Offer More Protection against COVID Than a Vaccine. Here's What Other Experts Say." CBC News, September 18, 2020, https://www.cbsnews.com/news/covid-face-mask-protection-vaccine-cdc-director/.

What utter psychopaths. They spend all day telling you to lose weight, eat better, and stop smoking, only to go out in the world and breathe hellfire into the universe.

Clearly, doctors should never, ever be able to take their masks off from now on, especially since we have learned so much cool "science" courtesy of coronavirus. Karen has reliably told us that we have to wear a mask so the virus doesn't jump the six degrees of separation between us and Kevin Bacon. And where did she hear it—from the experts, duh!

Consider doctors have been meeting with our comorbidity-riddled grandmas in their practices every single day every flu season to play Russian roulette while calling it "health care." Have they not a shred of decency? Have they not a scintilla of shame? Clearly nothing matters to these maskless monsters.

Does this not make any health care provider who wasn't wearing a mask 24/7 all these years whenever they ventured outside the home no better than a jihadist? Are we all clear on this? After all, it's just science. And the science, as always, is settled. Until it's a very fluid situation, of course.

We, the authors of this book, are shocked the same experts who finally figured out a man can have a uterus were so in the Dark Ages about the fact we beat the Black Death with masks. Can we get a witness? What a failure the

Hippocratic oath has been, not to mandate that doctors wear masks at all times all these years.

But seriously, folks, we used to be a culture that preached the Beatitudes. Now we are a culture obsessed with our fanaticisms.

One of the new fanaticisms is the mask, which has moved way, way, way, way past science and firmly into the realm of voodoo. Unfortunately, it's a voodoo that only gets more obnoxiously mandatory the more it is proven to be a total fraud.

Pardon our detour into sarcasm just now, but how else are we to respond to such fanaticism when there is absolutely nowhere masks have been shown in real time to be effective at slowing COVID after months and months of trying. No state. No country. Nowhere. And this was known not too long ago. In fact, we could write an entire separate book on just the maskerade, and what the real-time data says. But for the purpose of this discussion, here's a preview.

In May 2020, the CDC said "although mechanistic studies support the potential effect of hand hygiene or face masks, evidence from 14 randomized controlled trials of these measures **did not support a substantial effect** [emphasis added] on transmission of laboratory-confirmed influenza."[144]

On June 5, 2020, the World Health Organization said, "Many countries have recommended the use of fabric masks/face coverings for the general public. At the present time, the widespread use of masks by healthy people in the community setting is not yet supported by high quality or direct scientific evidence and there are potential benefits and harms to consider."[145]

A randomized study by the American College of Physicians Public Health Emergency Collection published on June 24, 2020, concluded "randomized trials in community settings found possibly no difference between N95 versus surgical masks and probably no difference between surgical versus no mask in risk for influenza or influenza-like (respiratory) illness."[146]

---

[144] Jingyi Xiao et al., "Nonpharmaceutical Measures for Pandemic Influenza in Nonhealthcare Settings—Personal Protective and Environmental Measures," *Emerging Infectious Diseases Journal* 26, no. 5 (May 2020), https://wwwnc.cdc.gov/eid/article/26/5/19-0994_article.

[145] "Mask Use in the Context of COVID-19," WHO, December 1, 2020, https://www.who.int/publications/i/item/advice-on-the-use-of-masks-in-the-community-during-home-care-and-in-healthcare-settings-in-the-context-of-the-novel-coronavirus-(2019-ncov)-outbreak.

[146] "Masks for Prevention of Respiratory Virus Infections, Including SARS-CoV-2, in Health Care and Community Settings," National Center for Biotechnology Information, June 24, 2020, https://www.ncbi.nlm.nih.gov/pmc/articles/PMC7322812/.

The University of Minnesota is host to the Center for Infectious Disease, which is directed by Dr. Michael J. Osterholm, who is now one of President Biden's coronavirus advisers. Osterholm's center published a commentary from two renowned respiratory virus experts on April 1, 2020, which made the case "masks-for-all for Covid-19 not based on sound data." It included the following analysis based on the volume of studies done on the topic prior to the politicization of COVID-19:

> *Sweeping mask recommendations—as many have proposed—will not reduce SARS-CoV-2 transmission, as evidenced by the widespread practice of wearing such masks in Hubei province, China, before and during its mass COVID-19 transmission experience earlier this year. Our review of relevant studies indicates that cloth masks will be ineffective at preventing SARS-CoV-2 transmission, whether worn as source control or as personal protective equipment.[147]*

Speaking of Osterholm, though he was singing a different tune at the time this book was being written, here's what he originally said about masks in an interview on June 12, 2020, right before mask fanaticism swept the country:

---

[147] Lisa M. Brosseau and Margaret Sietsema, "COMMENTARY: Masks-for-All for COVID-19 Not Based on Sound Data," Center for Disease Research and Policy," April 1, 2020, https://www.cidrap.umn.edu/news-perspective/2020/04/commentary-masks-all-covid-19-not-based-sound-data.

We now know that aerosols are a very critical way that influenza is transmitted just from talking, not coughing, or sneezing. We have increasing data that Covid is just like flu. You can achieve some of the same filtering as a N95 with a cloth mask. The problem is it's all about the fit. Unless it's a tight fit, it's like fixing three of the five screen doors on your submarine. The air just goes in the sides. I say if you don't have an N95 mask you aren't protected.

If you are walking across an intersection and a semi hits you at 50 miles-per-hour, that's not good. If you are walking across and a pick-up hits you at 50 miles-per-hour, that's still not good either. The outcome is the same. All the data says that just using a cloth mask may reduce the particles but not all. I would throw the kitchen sink at this if I thought it would make a difference but masks are not a major issue. In 1918 there were some exhaustive studies done on masks and not one found they made a difference.

Number two, just think common sense. The area of the world where we have the highest frequency of mask wearing in Nov and December of last year was China. Did that mask wearing make a difference? If you want to wear a mask, go ahead. I'm worried that people will assume a level of protection that they don't really have and put themselves in harm's way. If you don't wear a mask, we've come to make judgements about that on emotion.[148]

So why is Osterholm now singing a different tune? You'd have to ask him, but he's also not alone. Something radically changed in what we previously understood for years about the science of masks, and it just so happened to coincide with the spirit of the age anointing the mask as the talisman of its Branch Covidian jihad in the summer of 2020. It's truly a winter solstice miracle all these "studies" guaranteeing the mask's effectiveness just so happened to come out now, and continue coming in defiance of the real-time data that shows what we used to acknowledge as the truth about masks still is.

We're not saying, um, "science" knowingly determined to bow to the mob and abandon all its observable principles for political expediency, but did you know men can now have a uterus?

Dr. Harvey Risch of Yale University's School of Public Health (MD, PhD) summed up the ongoing maskerade with these words: "I honestly don't know how [anyone] could say masks are a lifesaving measure when there's no evidence to

---

[148] "Michael Osterholm—Masks, June 12, 2020," YouTube, June 27, 2020, https://www.youtube.com/watch?v=3CglBhn0znM.

suggest that. To call them a lifesaving measure is totally beyond the pale of anything that is scientific and knowable."[149]

While there's no evidence to support masks as a lifesaving measure, as Dr. Risch points out, there's plenty they are not.

Norway studied the effectiveness of mask mandates to slow the spread of COVID-19, and when it learned it would require forcibly masking 200,000 of its citizens to stop just one infection, the country determined it was pointless to ask anyone other than the symptomatic to wear them.[150] Florida, which has one of the highest elderly populations in the US as well as the third-largest population overall, assessed how counties that didn't have mask mandates performed versus those that did from May 1–December 15, 2020.[151] Here's what it found:

---

[149] Media Matters Staff, "Laura Ingraham and Guest Launch Conspiracy Theory Speculating That the COVID Vaccine Is a Plot to Sell More COVID Vaccines," Media Matters for America, February 25, 2021,
https://www.mediamatters.org/fox-news/laura-ingraham-and-guest-launch-conspiracy-theory-speculating-covid-vaccine-plot-sell-more.

[150] "200,000 Would Need to Wear Face Masks to Stop One New Infection: Norway Health Agency," The Local, June 11, 2020, https://www.thelocal.no/20200611/norway-doubles-down-on-no-face-mask-policy/.

[151] Len Cabrera, "After Nine Months, We Still Know Masks Don't Work," *Rational Ground*, https://rationalground.com/after-nine-months-we-still-know-masks-dont-work/.

> *22 of Florida's 67 counties have a mask mandate. There is essentially no difference in population-adjusted cases between masked and unmasked counties. Further, of the 20 counties that implemented a mask mandate after May 1, only three had a reduction in average daily cases.*[152]

Of course, it should be pointed out at least some of the indifference Florida saw in more than six months of real-time results could be attributed to voluntary mask usage or private businesses demanding them as a term of service even without a government mandate. For example, one of the coauthors of this book took his family to Orlando for a Disney vacation after the 2020 election, and masks were strictly enforced both indoors and outdoors there.

It should also be pointed out that those of us on the skeptical side of mask fanaticism are willing to grant such nuanced observations—rather than demand a slavish all-or-nothing compliance with a paint-by-numbers oversimplification there's no data to support. You know, like the maskholes do. But we're also not fanaticists, we're truth seekers.

Rational Ground also found similar indifference between case numbers and hospitalizations due to COVID between neighboring states, regardless of mask orders, when studying

---

[152] Len Cabrera, "After Nine Months."

these regions: North Carolina and South Carolina, [153] the DMV, [154] Pennsylvania and Delaware, [155] Mississippi and Alabama, [156] Washington and Oregon, [157] and California, Nevada, and Arizona.[158] A statewide review of coronavirus data in Kansas actually found lower infection rates in the ninety counties that didn't require masks compared to the fifteen that did.[159]

If you want to explain away all these indifferences due to voluntary mask usage and corporate sector compulsion all over the country, fine, but then you've also made the case that government mandates that at least flirt with tyranny really aren't necessary. You can't have it both ways. Either individuals and the corporate sector are able to deploy masks on their own and produce largely the same results as a government mandate, or the masks don't work whether it's the

---

[153] IM (@ianmSC), Twitter, December 23, 2020,
https://twitter.com/ianmSC/status/1341816261659873287.
[154] IM (@ianmSC), Twitter, December 19, 2020,
https://twitter.com/ianmSC/status/1340369604967759872.
[155] IM (@ianmSC), Twitter, December 19, 2020,
https://twitter.com/ianmSC/status/1340361186072690688.
[156] IM (@ianmSC), Twitter, December 18, 2020,
https://twitter.com/ianmSC/status/1340009590528700416.
[157] IM (@ianmSC), Twitter, December 16, 2020,
https://twitter.com/ianmSC/status/1339308172306071552.
[158] IM (@ianmSC), Twitter, December 15, 2020,
https://twitter.com/ianmSC/status/1338974424519692288.
[159] Dave Trabert, "More Deception: KDHE Hid Data to Justify Mask Mandate," *The Sentinel*, August 13, 2020, https://sentinelksmo.org/more-deception-kdhe-hid-data-to-justify-mask-mandate/.

public or private sector putting their faith in them. It's one or the other—choose.

However, voluntary mask usage and corporate compulsion don't explain preemptively feared super spreader events that don't fulfill the doomsday prophecies. Like Super Bowl LV, which was hosted by Tampa Bay, Florida, on February 7, 2021, and featured the hometown Buccaneers. The *Washington Post* was petrified as it observed "thousands of maskless Tampa fans flooded the streets, celebrating the Super Bowl win while risking a super spreader event."[160] But more than fourteen days later, which puts us past the pathological deadline for positive tests to indicate a so-called "super spreader" event actually occurred, daily new cases continued their steep downward slide in Hillsborough County, where the city of Tampa resides.[161]

Nor does it explain a CDC survey that reported a whopping 85 percent of those sampled who had been infected with COVID-19 claimed to be wearing a mask "always" or "often."[162] Those results aren't a surprise to those at the Centre

---

[160] Sam Amico, "Super Bowl Celebration Super Spreader? More Like Super Lies from the Media," OutKick, https://www.outkick.com/super-bowl-celebration-super-spreader-more-like-super-lies-from-the-media/.
[161] IM (@ianmSC), February, 21, 2021, https://twitter.com/ianmSC/status/1363540456269774848.
[162] Kiva A. Fisher et al., "Community and Close Contact Exposures Associated with COVID-19 among Symptomatic Adults ≥ 18 Years in 11 Outpatient Health Care Facilities—United States, July 2020," CDC, *Morbidity and Mortality*

for Evidence-Based Medicine at Oxford, the top-ranked university in the world. They could find no evidence cloth masks are effective against either COVID-19 transmission or infection.[163]

In February 2021, Swiss Policy Research set out to answer the question "are masks effective?"[164] It learned from the real-time data that "in many [European] states coronavirus infections strongly increased **after** mask mandates had been introduced [emphasis added]," and specifically noted that applied to Austria, Belgium, France, Germany, Ireland, Italy, Spain, and the United Kingdom.

Swiss Policy Research also found poison pills and fatal flaws in at least seven of the celebrated studies claiming masks are a COVID-19 panacea. Some of those errors included: the authors had to withdraw their study as infections and hospitalizations increased shortly after the study was published; comparing countries with very different infection rates and populations; the study actually used data from SARS-1 and was conducted in healthcare settings instead of

---

Weekly Report 69, no. 36 (September, 11, 2020), https://www.cdc.gov/mmwr/volumes/69/wr/pdfs/mm6936a5-H.pdf#page=4.
[163] Tom Jefferson and Carl Heneghan, "Masking Lack of Evidence with Politics," The Centre for Evidence-Based Medicine, July 23, 2020, https://www.cebm.net/covid-19/masking-lack-of-evidence-with-politics/.
[164] "Are Face Masks Effective? The Evidence." Swiss Policy Research, July 2020, updated February 2021, https://swprs.org/covid-masks-review/.

community settings; (and our personal favorite) "the review provided no real-world evidence supporting their proposition."

Fanatics typically don't need real-world evidence. Raw emotion is usually their preferred substitute. However, if you've lasted this long into this book you're like us—you want the truth. So let us march on to that end.

"The use of masks as part of a mask mandate for the general population didn't work when it was used to stop cases," said Dr. Scott Atlas of Stanford University, an advisor to former President Trump. "That's proven and it's not arguable. In Los Angeles County, Miami-Dade County, Hawaii, Alabama, the Philippines, Japan, the UK, Spain, France, Israel, and other places, the cases went up regardless and that's a fact. [Masks are] just one of the several obsessions that have happened during this pandemic. Honestly, it's an indication of how off the rails the whole discussion is."[165]

Science should be driven by neither obsession nor fanaticism, and when it is it ceases to be science. This was the warning issued by five Harvard-associated medical professionals writing in the *New England Journal of Medicine* on May 21, 2020, again before masks were politicized:

---

[165] "Dr. Scott Atlas UNLOADS on Lockdowns, Fake Science," *Steve Deace Show*, October 29, 2020, https://www.youtube.com/watch?v=QPuEU3I5_YI.

> *The chance of catching Covid-19 from a passing interaction in a public space is therefore minimal.... In many cases, the desire for widespread masking is a reflexive reaction to anxiety over the pandemic.... It is also clear that masks serve symbolic roles. Masks are not only tools,* **they are also talismans** *that may help increase health care workers' perceived sense of safety, well-being, and trust in their hospitals. Although such reactions may not be strictly logical, we are all subject to fear and anxiety, especially during times of crisis. One might argue that fear and anxiety are better countered with data and education than with a marginally beneficial mask, particularly in light of the worldwide mask shortage, but it is difficult to get clinicians to hear this message in the heat of the current crisis.[166] [emphasis added]*

In the course of our research for this chapter, we found numerous studies that previously proved masks are ineffective against respiratory viruses, especially those with airborne transmission such as COVID-19, which since have been updated to include a retconned disclaimer/warning/apology for daring to tell the truth during a previous era before the mask became the political talisman it is today. If that sounds like

---

[166] Michael Klompas et el., "Perspective: Universal Masking in Hospitals in the Covid-19 Era," *New England Journal of Medicine*, April 1, 2020, https://www.nejm.org/doi/full/10.1056/NEJMp2006372.

scientists begging the pardon of the mob for daring to do science, that's because it is.

As the maskerade continued on to the time we were writing this book, Dr. Atlas was even more blunt:

> *Mandating masks for the population does not stop cases. That is just super naïve, wrong, and just garbage science really. There is no real science to support that. The World Health Organization does not support that. That National Institute of Health does not support that. The CDC data itself shows that doesn't work. So that's sort of bordering on wearing a copper bracelet [to treat arthritis].*[167, 168]

Unfortunately, the tone for this maskerade was set from the get-go with Fauci's admitted dishonesty and antics. At the time we were writing this book, Fauci had devolved from telling us not to wear masks all the way to suggesting wearing two masks "just makes common sense."[169] And what was his evidence for such an obvious virtue signal claim? Why, an

---

[167] "Scott Atlas: I'm Disgusted and Dismayed," UnHerd, October 20, 2020, https://unherd.com/thepost/scott-atlas-im-disgusted-and-dismayed/.
[168] "Do Copper Bracelets Help Ease Arthritis?" Healthline, https://www.healthline.com/health/arthritis-bracelet.
[169] "Dr. Fauci: Double Masking against Mutant Coronavirus 'Just Makes Common Sense,'" *Today*, January 25, 2021, https://www.today.com/video/dr-fauci-double-masking-against-mutant-coronavirus-just-makes-common-sense-99959365958.

absolutely ridiculous CDC "study"[170] (and we use that term loosely) that double-masked mannequins! You know, inanimate objects that stay perfectly still and never have to breathe—unlike the rest of us actual humans. That is so mind-numbingly stupid (and obviously political), it's a total self-own they chose to do it with, well, dummies.

Proving once more that throughout this pandemic there has been one mask whose effectiveness cannot be questioned, and it's the one Fauci hides behind.

---

[170] Rachael Rettner, "CDC Says Double-Masking Improves Protection from COVID-19," LiveScience, February 10, 2021, https://www.livescience.com/cdc-double-masking.html.

Chapter 10

The Branch Covidian Cult

Throughout human history, our species has typically been prone to ignore potentially cataclysmic events in favor of comfort and carrying on with our daily lives. However, for perhaps the first time, a segment of the American population is bound and determined to turn COVID-19 into the apocalyptic event it never was.

That's not to say it is not in any way serious, for it most definitely is. COVID-19 is at least the worst pandemic to hit our nation since the Hong Kong flu in 1969, and maybe the worst since the Spanish flu of 1918. Which means it ranks somewhere between a midcentury and a once-a-century event. The loss of life, as well as the loss of way of life, makes this the most existential threat the average American has faced in their daily lives since Pearl Harbor.

Yet for a boisterous bloc of America that's not good...err...bad enough. They demand more, or worse. Anything less than World War Z simply won't cut it. Almost as if they crave apocalypse, and don't you dare try to take it away from them with something like the facts. To these people, any attempt at accurate reporting of the true infection fatality rate or case fatality rate, or daring to reassert the natural laws of science as it pertains to immunity, or daring to balance the broader socioeconomic fallout of mitigation efforts such as lockdowns, is akin to hate speech or you just hate old people.

For all intents and purposes, these Branch Covidians (as we call them) are perhaps the largest cult in American history. Every cult has a cult leader, and for these Branch Covidians their high priest is none other than Anthony Fauci.

Some of you may think describing these panic porn junkies as a cult is going too far, which is fair, so let's test that hypothesis. We believe there are seven characteristics of a cult. Let's go through them, one by one, and see how many of these boxes are checked by today's Branch Covidians.

1. **Cults discourage, if not outright oppose, critical thinking.** For crying out loud, must we even elaborate here on this very first one? The Branch Covidians not only refuse to consider any data that threatens their apocalyptic resolve, they seek to have others de-platformed and silenced for doing so. Only narratives that make COVID-19 out to be the love child of Ebola and smallpox are permitted through their Overton Window. Any treatments/remedies/solutions that

Donald Trump has ever spoken of fondly must immediately be discouraged or labeled as dangerous. And outside of when he's been forced to take questions from Senator Rand Paul a couple of times, you have rarely seen Fauci directly face any vetting of his views, regardless of how many times he contradicts himself. *Check*

2. **Cults isolate themselves and their members from the outside world, sometimes even forcibly.** This one is a little too on the nose as well, eh? All those lockdown fetishes, which is forcible isolation by the force of law. All those whose mantra was "I'm never coming out again until there's a vaccine." According to an Ohio State University poll, 72 percent of Americans still plan to wear masks in public even "after Covid-19 is no longer a threat." [171] In other words, most Americans still plan on at least partially isolating from the outside world long after a virus there's over a 99 percent chance they'll either never get or survive if they do is long gone. While we are skeptical the actual number of Americans still masking will be anywhere near that high when the time comes, and most of these

---

[171] Korin Miller, "Nearly Three-Quarters of Americans Still Plan to Wear Masks in Public after COVID-19 Is No Longer a Threat: Survey," Yahoo Life, February 9, 2021, https://www.yahoo.com/lifestyle/americans-still-plan-wear-masks-public-covid-19-no-longer-threat-survey-194043610.html.

respondents are likely virtue signaling to a pollster, what if it's only half that? That's still 36 percent, which is still well over a 100 million Americans. At the time we were writing this book, Fauci was out there telling Americans who had already been fully vaccinated they still needed to wear masks.[172] *Check*

3. **Cults claim to have special knowledge or that only the special can attain their knowledge.** The term "novel coronavirus" was meant to mean a new strain or variation of a familiar virus. For example, the term "coronavirus" is from the Latin word "corona" which means crown, and in the case of coronaviruses they were given this name because of the crown-like spikes on their surfaces.[173] But there are numerous types of coronaviruses,[174] including the type that cause the common cold, and we've been studying/fighting them in human beings since the 1960s. The coronavirus that causes COVID-19 is considered novel because the effects and complications it causes (such as the loss of

---

[172] "Fauci on Why You Should Still Wear a Mask after Vaccine," *Anderson Cooper 360*, CNN, February 18, 2021, https://www.cnn.com/videos/health/2021/02/18/dr-fauci-wear-mask-after-coronavirus-vaccine-sot-ac360-vpx.cnn.

[173] "Human Coronavirus Types," CDC, updated February 15, 2020, https://www.cdc.gov/coronavirus/types.html.

[174] Korin Miller, "Yes, the Common Cold Is Caused by Coronaviruses—Here's What You Should Know," *Prevention*, September 23, 2020, https://www.prevention.com/health/a34121295/common-cold-caused-by-coronavirus/.

a sense of smell) can differ from other coronaviruses. It is novel based on its behavior not its essence, which means the established/confirmed laws of virology, immunology, and biology remain intact. Which explains why, with a couple of symptomatic exceptions, it reacts and infects similar to other respiratory viruses. In fact, a study[175] from way back in May 2020 showed much of the population not yet infected with COVID-19 could already have what's called "crossover immunity," or a type of residual T-cell immunity because of past exposure to more common forms of coronaviruses. And a later study[176] showed T-cell immunity, a cellular immunity[177] that originates from T-cells in your bone marrow and isn't measured by your typical antibody test for a past/recovered infection, can last up to seventeen years after an infection from a coronavirus. How many Americans have likely been exposed to a coronavirus-driven common cold or other form of respiratory virus

---

[175] Daniel Horowitz, "Horowitz: Bombshell Study: Could Half the Uninfected Population Already Be Partially Immune?" TheBlaze, May 27, 2020, https://www.theblaze.com/op-ed/horowitz-bombshell-uninfected-population-immune.

[176] Daniel Horowitz, "Horowitz: New Study Shows 17 Years of Potential T Cell Immunity in SARS-Infected Patients," TheBlaze, July 16, 2020, https://www.theblaze.com/op-ed/horowitz-new-study-shows-17-years-of-potential-t-cell-immunity-in-sars-infected-patients.

[177] Ricki Lewis, "T Cells May Tell Us More about COVID Immunity," MedPage Today, November 18, 2020, https://www.medpagetoday.com/infectiousdisease/covid19/89777.

in the last seventeen years? Chances are quite a few, and this could be one of several reasons why a Johns Hopkins expert surprised many by recently predicting in the *Wall Street Journal* "we'll have herd immunity by (spring)."[178] Furthermore, a 2021 study from the National Institutes of Health found "lasting immunity" from a more conventional antibody perspective for those who had recovered from COVID-19, including the very promising finding "95% of the people had at least three of the five immune-system components that could recognize (Covid-19) up to eight months after infection."[179] Let's pause here for a moment and ask a question—how many of you reading this book have ever heard *any* of this information? How many of your friends, family, or neighbors have? Because without this type of information, you're going to assume "novel coronavirus" means an entirely whole new breed of virus the world has never seen before, therefore we have no baseline of precedent to go on when it comes to assessing how dangerous it is or what to do about it. Throughout this pandemic, including up to the time this book was being written, Fauci and his

---

[178] Marty Makary, "We'll Have Herd Immunity by April," *Wall Street Journal*, February 18, 2021, https://www.wsj.com/articles/well-have-herd-immunity-by-april-11613669731.

[179] Sharon Reynolds, "Lasting Immunity Found after Recovery from COVID-19," NIH Research Matters, January 26, 2021, https://www.nih.gov/news-events/nih-research-matters/lasting-immunity-found-after-recovery-covid-19.

ilk have abandoned numerous fundamentals of scientific precedent, including the crossover/T-cell immunity science[180] we just shared with you. Instead, Fauci and his knockoffs helped inspire this Branch Covidian cult by treating COVID-19 as if it were a blank slate, and of course you only fill in the blanks with the worst of the worst possibilities. *Check*

4. **Cults put loyalty to their leader above all else.** Google "trust Fauci" and you'll get over 10 million results (you'll get almost twice as many if you Google "I want to have sex with Anthony Fauci"). Google "in Fauci we trust T-shirt" and almost 1.7 million results come up, including 27 ads selling these shirts of various varieties. Google has listings for "in Fauci we trust" signs, socks, mugs, ornaments, bumper stickers, and (of course) masks. Etsy, a website that specializes in handmade or custom gifts, has numerous listings with the "trust Fauci" theme that boast thousands in sales apiece. *Saturday Night Live* canonized Fauci as a sex symbol.[181] *The Daily Show* wondered if Fauci was

---

[180] Erika Edwards, "Fauci, Paul Clash over Covid-19 Herd Immunity at Senate Hearing," NBC News, September 23, 2020, https://www.nbcnews.com/health/health-news/fauci-paul-clash-over-covid-19-herd-immunity-senate-hearing-n1240858.

[181] Dominic Patten, "'SNL' Gives Anthony Fauci the Full Sex Symbol Treatment as COVID-19 Vaccine Heats Up Cold Open," Deadline, December 12, 2020, https://deadline.com/2020/12/snl-coronavirus-vaccine-anthony-fauci-kate-mckinnon-cold-opener-1234655626/.

"the sexiest man alive."[182] CNN even acknowledged "the cult of Anthony Fauci"[183] and in a very on-brand take by the former news network, completely justified it. Famous actress Julia Roberts awarded Fauci with a "courage award" and while doing so told him, "You have been a beacon for us."[184] *Check*

5. **Cults seek to detach you from your families.** Chances are you're related to someone who will not tolerate any views on the virus beyond that which is spewed forth from Fauci's piehole. Chances are we've all been estranged from someone in our family because of lockdowns. Fauci told us not to have Thanksgiving in 2020 and proudly announced his own children wouldn't be coming home for the holiday that year.[185] Fauci also added later "for the first time in more than

---

[182] "Is Fauci Sexiest Man Alive?" *Daily Show with Trevor Noah*, April 17, 2020, https://www.youtube.com/watch?v=QlwDhjOmg4I.

[183] Chris Cillizza, "Explaining the Cult of Anthony Fauci," *The Point with Chris Cillizza*, CNN, April 20, 2020, https://www.cnn.com/2020/04/20/politics/anthony-fauci-poll-favorability-trump/index.html.

[184] Judy Kurtz, "Julia Roberts Presents Award of Courage to Fauci: 'You Have Been a Beacon for Us,'" The Hill, February 25, 2021, https://thehill.com/blogs/in-the-know/in-the-know/540490-julia-roberts-presents-award-of-courage-to-fauci-you-have-been.

[185] Will Feuer, "Dr. Fauci Says His Kids Aren't Coming Home for Thanksgiving as Americans 'Sacrifice' Holiday Gatherings to Stay Safe from Coronavirus," CNBC, October 14, 2020, https://www.cnbc.com/2020/10/14/dr-fauci-says-his-kids-arent-coming-home-for-thanksgiving-to-stay-safe-from-coronavirus.html.

30 years I'm not spending the Christmas holidays with my daughters."[186] To be fair, Fauci did say "it's very likely safe" for vaccinated family members to hug,[187] so he's not totally heartless. *Check*

6. **Cults cross moral boundaries and at times encourage others to as well.** While locking us down during "30 days to slow the spread" and demanding we stay away from friends and family, Fauci said random sex hookups with strangers you met online were totally kosher though.[188] However, taking the Eucharist at mass was not.[189] We've already documented in this book how many times he's either been dishonest or disingenuous. *Check*

7. **Cults separate you from the true church.** A survey of protestant churches by Lifeway Research in February 2021 found that even nearly a year since the

---

[186] Quentin Fottrel, "Dr. Fauci: 'For the First Time in More Than 30 Years, I'm Not Spending the Christmas Holidays with My Daughters,'" MarketWatch, December 16, 2020, https://www.marketwatch.com/story/dr-fauci-warns-of-dark-time-for-covid-19-after-christmas-and-hanukkah-surge-2020-12-08.

[187] Julia Musto, "Dr. Fauci: It's 'Very Likely' Safe for Vaccinated Family Members to Hug," Fox News, February 20, 2021, https://www.foxnews.com/health/dr-fauci-likely-safe-vaccinated-family-members-hug.

[188] Ben Cost, "Dr. Fauci Endorses Tinder Hookups 'if You're Willing to Take a Risk," *New York Post*, April 15, 2020, https://nypost.com/2020/04/15/fauci-endorses-tinder-hookups-with-a-caveat/.

[189] "Some Experts Split from Fauci on Holy Communion Recommendation," *Catholic Voice*, May 29, 2020, https://catholicvoiceomaha.com/some-experts-split-from-fauci-on-holy-communion-recommendation/.

pandemic began, in-person worship was still in decline. In fact, 11 percent *fewer* Protestant churches met in person in January 2021 than did in September 2020. That same survey found only 2 percent of Protestant churches had higher attendance in January 2021 than they did in January 2020, and only 30 percent say their attendance is back to normal.[190] From the Catholic perspective, Dan Cellucci of the Catholic Leadership Institute summed it up this way, "The pandemic has led to the acceleration of so many trend lines we were already on. What if they never come back?"[191] *Check*

The results speak for themselves. All seven boxes are checked. Not only is there really a Branch Covidian cult, with Anthony Fauci serving as high priest, but this could very well be the largest and most destructive cult in American history.

This now brings us to the antidote, or the seven steps to deconstructing this cult and its influence.

---

[190] Aaron Earls, "Fewer Churches Held In-Person Services in January," Baptist Press, February 22, 2021, https://www.baptistpress.com/resource-library/news/fewer-churches-held-in-person-services-in-january/.

[191] Claire Giangravé, "With Pews Emptied by COVID-19, a Catholic Researcher Asks, 'What if They Never Come Back?'" *America*, December 9, 2020, https://www.americamagazine.org/faith/2020/12/09/covid-mass-virtual-research-attendance-239433.

1. **Encourage critical thinking and seek out wisdom in a multitude of counsel.** There is so much research counter to Faucism out there that is easily accessible, just a morsel of which we have cited in this book. In addition, there are so many experts out there with exemplary résumés or from elite universities you can go to in order to think through this ordeal yourself. True, most of us are not qualified to confront COVID-19 as a health professional would, but we are by virtue of the US Constitution qualified to govern ourselves. The Founding Fathers entrusted this republic in the hands of "we the people" and not "them the experts" for a reason. We do most of the living, dying, and bill paying around here. Therefore, we get the final say. Be informed, yes, but be a citizen not a lemming.

2. **Take appropriate precautions, including vaccination if need be, but re-engage with the outside world.** Turn the TV off, and yes maybe even disengage from podcasts such as ours at times, too. There's a great big, beautiful creation out there, and some really neat people as well. Commit a subversive act, like shake hands with someone, and breathe the free air again. Get out of the COVID-bubble. Sure, bring the hand sanitizer and if you're running a temp or have recently been around someone who was stay home, but the vast majority of Americans face more

danger from isolation, depression, and financial loss due to COVID than they do COVID itself.

3. **Rely on established science.** The laws of immunology, biology, and virology were there for a reason. In times of fear, grifters appear. Like Eric Feigl-Ding, [192] for example. An unpaid visiting nutritionist at Harvard and long-time Democrat Party political operative, he suddenly became a media-quoted expert on coronavirus with a massive social media following by peddling ridiculous panic porn. He's hardly a lone wolf, and grifters like this are legion.

4. **Make the truth first and foremost.** Just because Trump trumpeted hydroxychloroquine doesn't make it bad, and just because you don't trust Trump doesn't by extension make Fauci holy. There have actually been plenty of times Fauci has said things the science agrees with, it's just that when he's done so it's too often also contradicted something he either previously said or will say later. But the truth is the truth, no matter its source. Nor is something true on the basis of the

---

[192] Jordan Schachtel, "The Impersonator: Eric Feigl-Ding, COVID-19, and an Implicit Far-Left Agenda," *The Dossier*, October 26, 2020, https://dossier.substack.com/p/the-impersonator-eric-feigl-ding.

convenience of accepting it. Results don't determine the truth; the truth determines results.

5. **Reunite with your families, again taking precautions if need be.** If you have someone in your family with autoimmune disease, diabetes, or other preexisting conditions COVID-19 preys upon, you may need to consider continuing with some mitigation efforts. But we were made to be more than a survival rate. Too many of our grandparents have died alone in the past year, without a final hug from their babies or grandbabies. And we're guessing almost every one of them would've chosen those final moments of love and affection over a few more weeks and months of oatmeal in seclusion. We were made for relationship, both with our Creator and one another. So go back to church to connect with Him and His people, and get back together to connect with one another. Be whole again.

6. **Cross the COVID fascism boundaries instead.** It is past time to defy, en masse, these Orwellian and mostly unenforceable (and ineffective) lockdowns. As feminist author Naomi Wolf (hey, remember we previously said the truth is the truth regardless of the source) eloquently said: "Nowhere in the Constitution does it say, all this can be suspended if there is a bad disease. We have lived through typhus, cholera,

smallpox, HIV, tuberculosis, polio, the Spanish flu. You know, we've lived through an attack on our soil. Never have there been months and months and months of emergency powers when we weren't actually fighting a war."[193] Amen, sister, praise the Lord and pass the civil disobedience. Open your businesses, your schools, and your churches. Those all belong to you. This is your country. Those are your communities. These are your children. Assert your God-given autonomy. We are not a nation of laws, and never have been. We are a nation of political will, and always will be. Therefore, you are in lockdown because you consent to it. The likes of Fauci are *never* giving you some magical "all clear." So stop consenting to this flat earth voodoo, and declare without apology that in this country the people rule once again.

7. **Put your trust in your faith, your family, and your freedom.** This is the trinity of American Exceptionalism. It sustained us through a War for Independence, a Civil War, two World Wars, a Cold War, an industrial revolution, past pandemics, civil

---

[193] "Naomi Wolf Sounds Alarm at Growing Power of 'Autocratic Tyrants,'" *Tucker Carlson Tonight*, Fox News, February 22, 2021, last update February 23, 2021, https://www.foxnews.com/transcript/naomi-wolf-sounds-alarm-at-growing-power-of-autocratic-tyrants.

unrest, and for more than two centuries. It can sustain us through COVID-19 as well.

Sadly, even if we follow all seven of these steps successfully, we will still have countrymen who refuse to leave the Branch Covidian compound of their own making. So be it. Kick the dust off your sandals, and move on with your way of life. If they choose to live their lives in fear, they have unfortunately made their choice.

But stop letting them choose for you.

Conclusion

"Those who would give up essential Liberty, to purchase a little temporary Safety, deserve neither Liberty nor Safety."

We began this book with an homage to arguably the most respected intellectual among our Founding Fathers, and that's also where we will now end it.

Benjamin Franklin was part of an American delegation sent to Great Britain in 1775 to try once more to negotiate with the oppressive King George III as tensions mounted and thoughts of revolution were being stirred. The argument being made by the British crown against the colonists at the time essentially came down to accept this tyranny in exchange for our "protection," so to speak. The taxes you pay without representation (or your consent) are for your protection. You are commanded to quarter the Red Coats, who are there for your protection (and to watch you), and so on and so forth. Basically a classic protection racket, right out of an old black-and-white mob movie. To which Franklin famously responded, "Those who would give up essential Liberty, to purchase a little temporary Safety, deserve neither Liberty nor Safety."

COVID-19 has taught us this history lesson in the harshest of terms. We consented to unprecedented government oppression and coercion in order to save as many lives as we could, and yet at the time this book was being finalized we were reporting over twenty-nine million cases and over a half million deaths anyway. We agreed to an unprecedented lockdown of the healthy out of fear they would asymptomatically kill our elderly, and still 95 percent[194] of all COVID-19 deaths were to people over the age of fifty anyway. Proving lockdowns don't work, but they do kill.

We also proved Franklin right. We gave up our liberty for a little safety, and we ended up with neither.

It is perfectly poetic, then, that at the time this book's writing was drawing to a close Anthony Fauci was presented a "courage award"[195] by a Hollywood actress who once starred in a movie called *Conspiracy Theory.* Now that's some straight-up schadenfreude right there. The conspiracy—whether premeditated or symbiotic—between the media and Fauci to endlessly fortify his messianic status is far more real

[194] Rachel Nania, "95 Percent of Americans Killed by COVID-19 Were 50 or Older," AARP, October 30, 2020, https://www.aarp.org/health/conditions-treatments/info-2020/coronavirus-deaths-older-adults.html.
[195] Michael Lee, "Julia Roberts Calls Fauci 'Beacon for Us" While Presenting Him with Courage Award," *Washington Examiner*, February 25, 2021, https://www.washingtonexaminer.com/news/julia-roberts-fauci-courage-award.

and spectacular than any actual medical or scientific expertise he has attempted to conjure.

We have never seen anything like it, despite the fact we cover politics for a living daily and are hardly innocent rubes. In our line of work you'll get lied to regularly, and that's when you're not being deceived. Still, the gaslighting empire Fauci has been permitted to preside over has even made our cynical jaws drop.

Because we have a biblical worldview and therefore understand mankind's depraved nature, we've warned our audience for years about the slippery slope that could deliver the likes of a Fauci from the depths of the swamp. That putting that much power in the hands of a sinner, as we all are, is just asking for trouble. We seem to think that once someone goes to work for the government they are no longer tempted like the rest of us, when the exact opposite is true. To have all that power and other people's money at your disposal, combined with so little accountability, is one of the main reasons why our Founding Fathers believed government was necessary to confront evil but should be limited lest it become the evil itself.

On our show we've also often predicted the circumstances under which such beloved false prophets could not only arise but be celebrated. Yet to actually have the front row seat to see it in real time, with clapping seals surrounding us on every side—as their rights, and their freedoms, and their virtue are obviously eroding with no end in sight—is simply stunning to behold. Like a tale of old, which is now our new normal.

We have lost so much of our heritage. Previous generations of Americans went to the mattresses when government told them how to live, but now we are sheeple who rise up and demand government not let us make our own decisions. "Come and take it" used to be an edgy patriotic dare referring to the Second Amendment. Now it's lamely and effeminately tweeted out by those who don't want government to ever end their futile mask mandates.

We used to encourage critical thinking. We now breed sheeple. Fauci exists in the minds of many such sheeple as the indispensable non-gendered-specific being in a year of madness, because he was primarily believed to be a calming and reasonable voice. Thus, he became the idol to be worshiped, particularly as he stood next to Donald Trump, the idol to be hated.

Results are secondary in a religion predicated on emotional validation. There are by now too many clearly documented hypocrisies, and changes of direction, for Fauci to be fawned over for producing any actual victories over coronavirus. But he didn't need those kinds of tangible results. He just needed to make the sheeple feel safe. Few really even try to spin Fauci as some kind of ultimate virus warrior as time goes on in any objective way, particularly in the press. They just claim him as a warm, fuzzy security blanket. He's the opposite of mean tweets, and for the Karen with the "coexist" bumper sticker in your suburban cul-de-sac, that's good enough.

Which, ironically, is just the cover Fauci required to become one of the most diabolical destroyers of self-governance and rugged individualism in all of American history. Whatever you think of Trump and his supporters, it is Fauci who has been the insurrectionist, while hiding in plain sight, since "15 days to flatten the curve" began and straight on through to its one-year anniversary. Whether in his heart of hearts he's truly motivated by an arrogant drive for attention or cruel-intentioned malice is irrelevant, because the outcome is malevolent just the same.

Our economy has been his plaything. Our emotions have been manipulated by him as if he's our Svengali. Our national history of taking on and solving big, existential problems has been shunned in favor of a self-defeating victimhood. Which at both a micro and macro level did more damage to American exceptionalism than all its spirit of the age predecessors could fever dream. If the likes of Fauci have their way, we'll soon be calling the virus "Afghanistan."

Along the way, Fauci has very rarely been held accountable in any meaningful sense or cross-examined with any degree of significance. And as free states like Florida, South Dakota, Georgia, and Iowa emerge as control groups to prove his beloved lockdowns aren't even a placebo but poison pills, they are either gaslighted by Fauci's sycophantic media enablers or memory-holed altogether to maintain the lie.

The lockdowns were the dumbest management decision in human history. The casedemic a fraud. The fear of hordes of asymptomatic carriers zombifying America flat-earth nonsense. All are narratives either propagated or perpetuated by Fauci. Governors like Kristi Noem in South Dakota, who prioritized hospitalizations and deaths first and foremost over raw numbers of positive tests, and Ron DeSantis in Florida who was among the first to end COVID-19 restrictions, have been proven right in their defiance of Fauci's pseudoscience. Fauci told Noem she'd have 10,000 of her people in the hospital, and she never had more than 600.[196] At the time this book was being written, Florida's COVID-19 hospitalizations among seniors (the most vulnerable demographic) had declined an incredible 80 percent![197]

Unlike Fauci, governors like these followed the actual science and balanced public health with overall public policy,

---

[196] Tré Goins-Phillips, "South Dakota Gov. Kristi Noem: 'Fauci Is Wrong a Lot,'" Faithwire, March 1, 2021, https://www.faithwire.com/2021/03/01/south-dakota-gov-kristi-noem-fauci-is-wrong-a-lot/.
[197] Kyle Lamb (@kylamb8), Twitter, March 2, 2021, https://twitter.com/kylamb8/status/1366788924358746112.

and they now have the results to show they were right. Their people are healthier, medically *and* socio-economically, than whatever is going on inside Fauci's beloved New York by far. But to the sheeple who would rather not make decisions for themselves, or self-govern, it doesn't matter. Fauci's serene façade is a come hither, and they can't wait to rub the monkey's paw or apply yet another mask. They get off on being his submissive.

However, behind Fauci's serene façade the man is an unrelenting agent of chaos. Think Sir Patrick Morgan from the movie *Wonder Woman*. He's as kindly and seemingly thoughtful as they come from his perch in the British War Cabinet during World War I. The guy you put there to keep the hawks from going too far and the doves from never finding their courage. Sober through and through. A true plumb line.

But we all now know that, speaking of masks, Sir Patrick doesn't truly embody any of that at all. For he is actually Ares, the God of War, and he means to manipulate events in whatever way he deems necessary to grab more and more of the spotlight that he both craves like a drug and ardently believes he is uniquely entitled to.

Sound eerily familiar, maybe?

Well, let's just put it this way: if you put the Lasso of Truth around Fauci to find out what his true motivations are, you're not likely to rush out and buy a "trust Fauci" T-shirt right afterwards.

The Branch Covidian cult notwithstanding, increasing skepticism and even anger about the longstanding COVID-19 advisory role of Fauci has also filled social media in the days this book was being completed. Sure, some of us have been pointing out the need to rid the White House and the nation of his presence for nearly a year now, but turns out Fauci's latest calls for double masking and remaining locked down even after getting vaccinated pushed a new segment of Americans over the edge.

To that we say what took you so long, and Amen!

The army grows of those people who simply, for an untold number of reasons both selfish and profound, want their damn country back and resent that the so-called "experts" seem to be addicted to either doubling down on failure, or mandating increasingly hysterical and obtuse remedies that would make Rube Goldberg machines blush.

It's a lot more than mere resentment, though. So many people have been hurt in mind, body, and soul by Fauci's arrogant and inconsistent medical meanderings as life has been turned into a "Wipeout" obstacle course without any of the belly laughs. You say you want to merely provide for your family and your employees, Ms. Texas hairdresser? Straight to jail for you.[198]

You simply want to worship God and speak freely by singing hymns per the guarantees of the First Amendment of the United States Constitution, you rascally Idaho protestors? You are under arrest.[199]

You desire for your kids to be educated, Washington State band parents? Enjoy your bubble.[200]

Our ability to trust one another as fellow citizens to be rational and decent is in tatters. It might be years before we realize how busted we truly are, as both individuals and a community, because of Fauci's and others' perverse Frankenstein act. The claim that he is a healer is a farce that grows days by day. Instead, he has specialized in growing hopeless zombies and goose-stepping minions in his lab of nonsense.

---

[198] Paul J. Weber and Jake Bleiberg, "Texas Salon Owner Jailed for Defying Governor's Order Freed," Associated Press, ABC News, May 7, 2020, https://abcnews.go.com/Health/wireStory/governor-softens-order-jailed-texas-hair-salon-owner-70555611.

[199] Ezra Dulis, "Idaho Police Arrests 3 at Outdoor Church Worship Event in Defiance of Mask Mandate," Breitbart, https://www.breitbart.com/faith/2020/09/24/idaho-police-arrest-3-at-outdoor-church-worship-event-in-defiance-of-mask-mandate/.

[200] Jason Duaine Hahn, "Wash. High School Gives Band Students Individual Bubbles to Curb COVID Spread in Viral Photo," *People*, February 25, 2020, https://people.com/human-interest/washington-high-school-band-practices-in-green-bubbles-protect-against-covid/.

There needs to be accountability after a year of such needless overreach and arrogance. Somebody has to pay. We need a 9/11 style of tribunal to get to the bottom of this hellscape. Because this all could have been different if we'd learned the right lessons nearly a year ago, when yet another casualty of chaos like Idaho's Sara Brady was among the first to fall victim to Fauci's paranoia-inducing spell.

She's the mom who was arrested in April 2020[201] for the high crime of playing on a playground with her kids and now continues to wait in limbo for a trial to address her trespassing charge as she amasses growing attorney fees. Brady had been at the park for barely five minutes before police arrived at the behest of a Karen Supreme, who simply couldn't tolerate the freedom being enjoyed right in front of her as she cowered in her car eating lunch. And so it was that two young children saw their mother handcuffed right in front of them by the inheritor of Barney Fife's limp pistol and tin can badge.

"Unfortunately for the officer and the state of Idaho, they arrested a woman who will fight until she has no breath left in her," said Tim Brady, Sara's husband, when we interviewed him. "What a lot of people don't know, especially those that have taken time out of their lives to criticize, threaten, harass,

---

[201] Snejana Farberov, "Moment Idaho Mother-of-Four, 40, Is Arrested for Using Closed Playground, Sparking Mass Anti-Lockdown Protest," *Daily Mail*, April 22, 2020, https://www.dailymail.co.uk/news/article-8245221/Idaho-mom-arrested-protesting-coronavirus-lockdown-closed-playground.html.

and stalk her and our family, is that she is ironically the wife of a police officer. To add insult to injury, I have worked with the officer that arrested my wife several times throughout my 19-year law enforcement career."

Yeah, you heard that right. A cop is so fed up with the abuses of power destroying our nation that he is now speaking up without apology. Because this is about far more than just his wife. Fauci isn't supposed to be our model or our muse for how government works, or how America's citizens are to be respected and served.

"I have to hope that law enforcement's role with the tyrannical orders and edicts over the past year are the minority," Tim said. "I fear that the profession I love will someday in the future force me to leave because I won't participate in destroying my nation. The next time you hear or see a story about the abuse of law enforcement power, please remember there are those of who are still out there fighting for what is right. Vowing to uphold the oaths we have taken."

This is the chaos and purposelessness Fauci and company have wrought as whatever oaths they once took, Hippocratic or otherwise, have been forgotten or perverted. Where a cop's faith in his noble profession, as well as his own respect for authority, is hanging by a very slim thread as he watched roughly four hundred inmates released from his local county prison due to COVID—only to then make room behind bars for the likes of his sweet wife for daring to get some fresh air.

Every bit of it is insane, but it keeps happening over and over again because too many people have remained drunk on a cocktail mix of relative comfort, denial, cowardice, and sloth to do anything about it. This is, of course, not unique before times of great pillaging and conquest throughout human history, but it is then all the more remarkable that we refuse to now see what is going on before our eyes.

One of the most memorable chapters this book's authors have ever read comes early in Elie Wiesel's gut-wrenching Holocaust memoir *Night*. He describes the level of disbelief, deflection, excuse-making, and wish-casting that prevented so many—Jews and Gentiles alike—from truly grappling with the inevitable horror that was ramping up before them, no matter how bad the rumors of the gas chambers got or the increasing weight of the Nazi boot on the throat became.

Wiesel is describing people who have been slow-boiled in a pot, frog-like, so that they never make the determination that it is a matter of life and death to jump out. It is a world in which the weight of the truly existential and virtuous has been minimized or marginalized to such an extent that the worst-case scenarios simply seem to be impossible. And if somebody does ring a bell of caution, it is seen as weird or extreme or even criminal.

The thing is, spend enough time not dwelling on the fundamentals that make any society worthy of having, let alone capable of being passed on from generation to generation, and the impending darkness inevitably can't or won't be seen in the appropriate cautionary context. But the darkness comes nonetheless and is no less savage for it. Often the worst forms of darkness originally come to us as bringers of light.

Which brings us back to Fauci. It doesn't really matter in some respects how self-aware he is about his culpability in seducing America into a similar spiral of chaos, mayhem, and (hat tip to Orwell) unpersoning unreality. Where airline personnel are so concerned about social distancing they reportedly slap each other five to congratulate themselves for "a job well done to those Jews." All because one Jewish baby wasn't wearing a mask on the flight.[202]

The fact remains that Fauci is at the heart of this heart of darkness poised to consume us as a people if not ended soon, whether that is by design or by accident. He is both the Branch Covidian tribal shaman and the prime minister of Covidstan. Few have ever had so little accountability for their inadequacy

---

[202] Ben Sales, "Frontier Accused of Kicking Hasidic Family Off Flight Due to Unmasked Toddler," *The Times of Israel*, March 2, 2021, https://www.timesofisrael.com/frontier-accused-of-kicking-hasidic-family-off-flight-due-to-unmasked-toddler/.

in addressing the task at hand, while being handed so much unconstitutional and unwarranted responsibility for doing so.

What was irresponsible at the beginning cruised straight into irrational and now firmly resides in the irreverent. We at nearly every turn have seemingly been stripped of even a basic ability to prefer the good, the true, and the beautiful when measured against the despotic comforts of the experts who will make all your wildest dreams come true—by recasting them as the vision quest of their own societal fetishes.

Our fear has gifted such authority to Fauci. So even if his lust for fame and power and validation becomes more acutely absurd by the day, it only seems to reinforce his status as savior because for us to consider otherwise would be to admit our partial authorship of this entire grift. Fauci only sold much of America what it wanted to buy, and even now that his documented failure is complete he still has plenty of buyers. And even if there never was an Anthony Fauci to buy it from, too many Americans would've just found another snake oil vendor. The heart wants what the heart wants.

For God's sake, enough.

Fauci isn't your friend. He's a fiend. Franklin was one of our beloved Founding Fathers, but Fauci is an unfounding deadbeat dad. Nearly every premise he has asserted from the beginning has either been a well-intentioned or purposeful undermining of truth, the Constitution, the rule of law,

174

common decency, and individual liberty. A year under Fauci's thumb makes King George III's madness look like the JV team, and that's not even talking about the mental health cataclysm that awaits. His time as the Wormtongue-esque shadow casting a pall over our nation must come to an end. But for that freedom to return, our own fear that has become our idol has to go.

Time to throw that idol into the fire…

About the Authors

Steve Deace and **Todd Erzen** team up for the Steve Deace Show each weekday for The Blaze. They both live in Iowa with their wives and children. This is Deace's seventh book he's either written or co-authored, and Erzen's first. Both of them had a background in newspaper reporting before crossing over into broadcasting.

Also by Steve Deace

A Nefarious Carol

Truth Bombs: Confronting the Lies Conservatives Believe (To Our Own Demise)

A Nefarious Plot

Rules for Patriots: How Conservatives Can Win Again